THE SEARCH FOR
'GESTAPO' MÜLLER

THE SEARCH FOR 'GESTAPO' MÜLLER

THE MAN WITHOUT A SHADOW

by

CHARLES WHITING

LEO COOPER

First published in Great Britain 2001 by
LEO COOPER
an imprint of
Pen & Sword Books Ltd
47 Church Street
Barnsley
South Yorkshire
S70 2AS

ISBN 0 85052 774 0

A catalogue record of this book is
available from the British Library

Typeset in 11/13pt Candida
by Phoenix Typesetting, Ilkley, West Yorkshire

Manufactured in the USA

CONTENTS

ACKNOWLEDGEMENTS

With many thanks to my son Julian; Mr Carl Sillitoe, College of Ripon and St John, York; Mr Wolfgang Trees (Aachen): Professor H. Morris (Springfield N.Y.); Tom Dickinson (New York City); Colonel Hunton Downs, USA, retd; *Staatsanwalt* Wicker, *Zentrale Stelle der Landesjustizverwaltungen* (Ludwigsburg); Simon Wiesenthal Center: Haifa Document Centre.

Also with thanks to the eyewitnesses, now mostly dead: Otto Skorzeny, Albert Bormann, Otto Strasser, L. Heydrich, P. Hanfstaengl, ex- *Gauleiters* Florian, Wahn, Jochen Peiper, Jochen von Lang (*Stern*), Heinz Hoehne (*Spiegel*).

C.W.

'The facts are now clear, and if myths, like the truth, depend on evidence, we are safe. But myths are not like truth; they are the triumph of credulity over evidence. The form of a myth is indeed externally conditioned by facts; there is a minimum of evidence with which it must comply if it is to live, but once lip-service has been paid to that undeniable minimum, the human mind is free to indulge in its infinite capacity for self-deception.'

Hugh Trevor-Roper (Lord Dacre), 1947.

INTRODUCTION

'The tales of that time . . . speak only of self-sacrifice, patriotic devotion, despair, grief – heroism. But it was not really so. . . . Most people at the time paid no attention to the general progress of events, but were guided only by their private interests.'

Leo Tolstoy

It was dark when they reached Berlin that night over sixty years ago. The November air was cold, but the kidnapped Englishman was sweating. The heater in the Mercedes which had carried him from the German border with neutral Holland, where the SS had kidnapped him, had been turned up full blast. Besides, the heavily armed thugs, half his age, who guarded him had chained him up and kept a thick hood over his head most of the time. Indeed, he had almost passed out for a while. Now they pushed and shoved him up the steps into Number Ten Prinz Albrecht Strasse, which, he already knew, was the headquarters of the Gestapo. Minutes later, still handcuffed, he was sitting on a blue couch, facing a small German who called himself 'Doctor Max'. The English prisoner didn't think that was his real name. Germans of his lower-middle-class sort, he told himself in his snobbish manner, loved to give themselves fake academic titles.*

---

* See C. Whiting: *The Venlo Betrayal* (Pen & Sword) for further details.

1

Still, the fellow seemed reasonable enough. He told the kidnapped man, 'Do calm yourself, Mr Best. Nothing will happen to you if you will only be reasonable. But remember you are in our power and if you won't behave yourself we shall have to adopt very different measures with you.'

Best, a British spy, wasn't impressed. Could he have a wash and shave? This set 'Dr Max' off shouting and bullying, but it didn't have the effect he expected. Best was used to Germans; he'd been buying them and using them for espionage purposes against their own country for nearly a quarter of a century. He knew their tactics. Later Best reported, 'I found Dr Max a very pleasant little man who paid me the compliment of always laughing at my jokes.' Not now, however. So Best said, 'If you're going to shoot me, why not go ahead?'

That took the wind out of Max's sails. He went into the next room and appeared a little later with his chief, 'a dapper, exceptionally good-looking little man, dressed in imitation of Adolf Hitler, in a grey uniform jacket, black riding breeches and topboots. He started to "snort"* immediately he entered and, as he walked towards me, increased the pitch of his voice with great virtuosity.'

Mr Best was not impressed. Nor did the little man's next threat frighten him particularly. The German shouted at him, 'You are in the hands of the Gestapo. Don't imagine we shall show you the slightest consideration. The Führer has already shown the world that he is invincible and soon he will come and liberate the people of England from Jews and plutocrats such as you. It is war and Germany is fighting for her existence. You are in the greatest danger and if you want to live another day you must be very careful.'

According to Best, 'He then sat down on the chair in front of me and drew it up as close as possible, apparently with the intention of performing some mesmerizing trick. He had rather funny eyes which he could flicker from side to side with

---

* *Anschnauzen*, to cry at someone in a threatening manner. Best translated it as 'to snort'.

2

the greatest rapidity and I suppose that this was supposed to strike terror into the heart of the beholder.'

But with typical English phlegm, Best replied coolly, 'I have something the matter with my eyes too. Could I perhaps have my glasses?'

Naturally the little man went off the handle at this. Being a German, he couldn't understand English wit. 'Don't you worry about glasses. You will probably be dead before morning and then you won't need glasses . . . or anything else. You don't seem to realize your position. It is war. You are no longer an honoured guest of Germany, but a prisoner of the Gestapo. Don't you know where you are? You are in the headquarters of the Gestapo. Don't you know what that means? We can do anything we like with you. *Anything!*' *

Thus, half a century ago, the Western reading public was introduced to SS General Heinrich Müller, head of the German *Geheime Staatspolizei* (Gestapo), for the first time. Although, at the end of this first interview with the captured British Secret Intelligence Service (SIS) chief, Müller said in an almost friendly voice, 'Give Mr Best what he wants,' he certainly did come across as a very frightening man. As indeed he was. He had to be. For in that year, 1950, Müller was Number Two on the list of 120,000 wanted Nazi criminals, still being actively sought by the allies. Ahead of him, as Number One was *Reichsleiter* Martin Bormann, Hitler's vanished 'Brown Eminence'. Behind Müller as Number Three was SS Colonel Adolf Eichmann, the executor of the 'Final Solution'.

Thereafter the media remained almost totally silent about the fate of the Reich's Number Two War Criminal. Even though his case is still on the books of the German Ministry of Justice to this day, no one seems interested.

Müller, although he became an SS general, remained a shadowy figure throughout his quarter-century career as a policeman. During the Nazi period he kept in the background, concerning himself with professional police work and

* Captain Payne Best: *The Venlo Incident*, Hutchinson (1950).

3

not with the 'Final Solution', although he was present at the infamous Wannsee Conference of 1942. Only rarely did he allow his photograph to be taken. In that, he was wise, cautious and very professional. The cop who had persecuted the Nazis vigorously while they had been in opposition had learned his lesson. In 1933, when they came to power, his career had been almost destroyed. Thereafter he kept a low profile.

Müller's case, after he was last seen alive on 29 April 1945 in Hitler's Berlin Bunker, was also overshadowed by the fates of Martin Bormann and Adolf Eichmann. Eichmann was in the limelight for 15 years until the Israelis finally kidnapped him in South America and put him up for trial. And it was nearly 20 years before Martin Bormann was at last declared dead by the German government. In that time the media paid no attention to Müller's fate, even though he was still possibly on the run into the '80s, even '90s. As late as 1997 the US publishing house, Simon & Schuster, for instance, paid a reported £500,000 to an author who maintained that Bormann had been smuggled into Britain by Ian Fleming, the creator of '007', and a team of commandos. The supposed intention was to help the British recover a fortune in Nazi gold stashed away in Swiss bank accounts. Bormann was said to have lived in, of all places, Reigate, Surrey.*

Perhaps another reason for the apparent lack of interest in the whereabouts of the missing Chief of the Gestapo, who had been the authorizing power behind all the atrocities committed between 1939–1945 throughout Nazi-occupied Europe, including murders of the British SAS, Paras and Commandos and the fifty POWs shot in the 'Great Escape', the movie of which is regularly shown on Christmas TV, was his supposed refuge after 1945.

It was Russia, and at the height of the Cold War the KGB would allow no *Sunday Times*-type investigative reporting

* Ironically enough, the same US publishing house had paid another foreign author, American-Hungarian Ladislas Farago, another huge sum for 'proving' that he had met Bormann living in 1972 in the South American jungle. Bormann certainly got around.

there, that was for sure. Indeed many so-called authorities on Müller's fate suggested he might well have been a leading member of that organization himself by that time.

It was probably SS General Schellenberg, the *Wunderkind* of the German Intelligence who worked closely with Müller throughout the war, who set the ball rolling at the time of his death in exile in 1952. By then a longtime tool of the British Secret Intelligence Service (SIS), who had appeared as a witness at the trial of the major war criminals such as Goering, Ribbentrop and the like, he recorded the most significant conversation he ever had with the feared Gestapo Chief some time in 1943.

Müller was drunk and unusually talkative. He began to talk about the Red Orchestra [the Russian spy ring]. He occupied himself with the motives for these treason cases and the intellectual background from which they stemmed. 'National Socialism,' Müller pronounced thickly, 'is nothing more than a sort of dung on this spiritual desert [Germany]. In contrast to this one sees that in Russia a unified and really uncompromising spiritual and biological force is developing.'

With an attempt at humour, the much younger Schellenberg joked, 'All right, let's all start saying "Heil Stalin" right now, and our Little Father* Müller will become head of the NKVD.†

Müller was not amused. 'That would be fine,' he slurred. 'You'd really be for the high jump, you and your diehard bourgeois friends.'

At the time Schellenberg was puzzled: 'I still couldn't work out what Müller was driving at, but I was enlightened later.'

Indeed he was, as were all those who had been involved in German intelligence and had had dealings with Müller. They concluded that he had been working secretly for the Russians all along. From 1933 onwards, when he was accepted into the Gestapo, he had been a 'mole' in Himmler's security *apparat*. In the end he had worked himself right to the top as the head of the Gestapo and had been familiar with most of the Reich's deepest secrets. As SS Colonel Skorzeny, that fanati-

* Russian usage for the Soviet dictator Stalin.
† The then Russian Secret Police and equivalent of the Gestapo.

5

cal Nazi who had once rescued Hitler's friend and fellow dictator Mussolini from his mountain jail, said, 'Müller, in fact, betrayed us all.'[*]

Thus for nearly thirty years Müller was relegated to the no-go area, as far as the media was concerned. He'd gone over to the Russians and that was that. But once the Wall came down and the Soviet Empire began to crumble, there was renewed interest in wartime treachery, especially by those who had possibly worked for the Russians. Former KGB agents were selling their souls, and their grandmothers, for hard currency. In the States the authorities had their hand forced. They had to de-classify more and more of the 'Venona Files' dating from the murky period when Soviet Intelligence had 'moles' and agents right at the very top, including the assistant to General 'Wild Bill' Donovan, the head of the war-time OSS, the forerunner of the CIA!

But even in the early '90s, when the Soviets and their successors in the new Russian Republic were selling virtually everything of their secret intelligence past for dollars, nothing was ever discovered about what had happened to Müller. Even as I write, the Moscow authorities have put on display secret artefacts relating to the last days of Adolf Hitler, artefacts which have been hidden for over five decades. But of Germany's sole remaining major war criminal *nothing*!

So what did happen to SS General Heinrich 'Gestapo' Müller? This book is a modest attempt to answer that question.

[*] To the author.

I

THE MAKING OF A MONSTER

And many more Destructions played
In this ghastly masquerade.
All disguised even to the eyes,
Like Bishops, lawyers, peers or spies.

Shelley

1945: MÜLLER'S LAST CASE

'The Führer is dead. . . . It's every man for himself.'

Sergeant Tornow, Kennelman at the Führerbunker
upon hearing of Hitler's suicide, 30 April 1945.

ONE

At five minutes after midnight on the morning of Monday 23 April 1945 the order was issued. It was *Clausewitz*. A single word, the name of that long-dead Prussian general who had written the most famous treaties on war in the whole history of human conflict. Perhaps an apt choice. For General Clausewitz had helped to rally a hard-hit German nation when it was at the point of despair.

The order came from the headquarters of the city's battle commandant and it was timely. The Red Army's assault troops were smashing their way ruthlessly towards its inner circle. Both the Stettin Railway Station and the 'Alex'*, as it was known, were under attack. To the south Marshal Koniev's troops had broken through. In essence the capital was surrounded, save at a few points to the west.

Now the teleprinters began clacking urgently. The 'Lightning Girls' (*Blitzmädchen*) sprang into action. Following the lists pinned above their heads in the underground, sandbagged telephone exchanges, they began their rounds. Telephones rang all over the city. Staff officers ran back and forth with check-lists. Dispatch riders bearing heavy leather pouches and Schmeisser machine pistols slung across their chests ran for their machines.

From shattered ministries, Party headquarters and military

---

* Alexanderplatz.

11

command posts the secret code-word flashed back and forth, even to those parts of the city now held by the Russians. 'Clausewitz! Clausewitz! *CLAUSEWITZ!*' In the state offices, Party sub-sections, regimental and battalion head-quarters, police, fire brigade and Gestapo posts, the safes were opened and the sealed envelopes with their legend in red *'Staatsgeheimnis'* (State Secret) were torn open.

Some were shocked by what they read. Others were on the verge of tears. Many realized at once that this what they had long been waiting for: it was time for them to do a bunk. A few fanatics jutted their jaws, tapped their belts to reassure themselves that their pistols were still there and told them-selves that if they were going to go down they'd take a few of the Red slime-shitters with them.

By the time dawn came, most of the three million civilians and soldiers in the beleaguered city knew their fate. As the first salvoes of the now customary Russian 'hate' began, smashing into the ruins, they had heard the dread message revealed by the code-word 'Clausewitz'.

All senior civilian officials, ministerial and Wehrmacht staffs, were to break out of the ruined city immediately and head west to North Germany or south through the Russian and American lines to the Bavarian-Austrian mountains. Their places would be taken by the troops already heading for the capital in force to take over the defence. As SS Doctor Ernst-Guenther Schenk, who, as a 44-year-old, had volun-teered from a cushy job in one of the ministries to stay behind with a combat battalion, was to put it: 'We Berliners are to stay. *Clausewitz* ensures that the city will be defended and the enemy defeated. The strong hands of the Führer will ensure that everything will be all right, for *he* always plans well in advance.'

But on this day when the decision to defend Berlin was announced Schenk, a brave man who would suffer ten years in a Soviet hell-camp because of that decision, asked himself the same question that many Berliners were asking that Monday: 'But where *is* the Führer?'

Unlike his implacable enemy, 'that drunken old sot'

Churchill, Adolf Hitler detested wasting time on the Home Front. He never visited bombed German cities, attended sittings of his rubber-stamp parliament, *the Reichstag*, or consoled the men who had given their lifeblood for him in the military hospitals back in the Reich. Almost throughout the whole war, the Führer remained, as far as the German populace was concerned, the invisible man. He liked to give the impression that he was constantly at the front, especially in the East, leading the battle against Soviet Russia. What the average German knew of their Führer came from his radio broadcasts and the film reports of him at the front, courtesy of the *Deutsche Wochenschau* (official newsreel).

Now, on this Monday when a confused and frightened Berlin populace asked itself where exactly the Führer was, they would have been greatly surprised to find that he was in their midst. In fact he had been in the capital since virtually the end of Germany's last gamble in the West, the abortive Ardennes counter-attack. Not that many of his 'loyal Berliners', as he liked to call them, could ever have hoped that terrible spring to see their leader in their native city. For on that fateful Monday when the final phase began, Adolf Hitler, the 'Great Captain of All Times', spent most of his time beneath their feet. He was sitting out the end of the war, impotently hiding in the great bunker underneath the shattered wreck of the Reich Chancellery.

Hitler had gone to ground nearly two months before. He had returned from the failed Ardennes Offensive a broken man, not only in health, but in mind and spirit too. Now he was bent, grey and shaking. He dragged one leg in a bad limp and cradled one arm in his other, using his good hand to raise and lower the bad one. On 20 April he had celebrated his last birthday and those guests who knew him of old and had toasted him in champagne had told themselves that he looked twenty years older than his actual age. His colour, metabolism and pinched face were those of a dying man. Even that 'meteorism' which they had all feared seemed to have vanished.

But for those close advisers still confined with him in his

red-carpeted private bunker, adorned with a single portrait, that of Frederick the Great in a French powdered wig, the Führer's most frightening and unsettling ailment was his mind. It seemed to have gone, at times almost completely so.

He ranted and raved. He commanded imaginary armies and issued orders to those which no longer existed or were in the process of breaking up. When the pressure was too much, he grew violent, and threatened dire penalties to both friend and foe, though he had no means of carrying out such threats, even if his generals had passed them on.

One day earlier that April, when he heard that Allied radio had reported that German troops had rescued US air bomber crews shot down and about to be lynched by angry towns-folk, he turned to General Koller of the *Luftwaffe* and cried, as if he didn't believe his own ears, 'Koller, I order that all bomber crews shot down these last few days be turned over to the SD [Security Service] and liquidated.' Later he button-holed Koller and SS General Kaltenbrunner, head of the SS's security services, on the same subject: 'What am I to do against this nightmare terror-bombing and murder of our women and children?' Again he thundered that Allied bombing crews would have to be 'liquidated as terrorists, then they'll think twice about whether to fly over Germany'.

Naturally neither Koller nor Kaltenbrunner, who was already planning to make his own escape from the Bunker, attempted to carry out this crazy order. They didn't want to be executed as war criminals after the war which *they* knew was already lost.

By mid-April the Führer's outbursts had increasingly been occasioned by seemingly unimportant incidents. As Captain Beermann, one of his SS bodyguards, stated later, 'After 16 January Hitler never saw another sunrise or sunset. He worked, slept, took meals and tea, bathed, made his toilet, married and died, all underground. In a world where day and night blended into a continuous glare of artificial light, the departure from reality was to become more evident with each passing week.'

In his last conversation with SS General Gottlob Berger, known throughout the SS as 'the Duke of Swabia' on account of his grand manner, Hitler 'raved like a madman'.* Listening to the captive General, the Secret Service agents heard him describe the Führer in those last days in the Bunker 'as a raving paranoid madman, who blamed everyone around him for the demise of the Third Reich.' He screeched at Berger before his wise departure for safer climes: 'Everyone has deceived me. No one has told me the truth. The Armed Forces have lied to me. Finally the SS has left me in the lurch.'

This feeling of betrayal seemed in those last days to be part and parcel of Hitler's paranoid insistence that there was a spy inside the underground chambers, a leak right at the top. As Speer, his Minister of Armaments, recorded after the war: 'In those last weeks in the Bunker, a special phenomenon of Hitler's mind was a kind of trigger reaction. When he started in on the theme of treason and treachery, he would usually remark, "This all began with that idiot Rudolf Hess." He would then couple Hess's defection with the 20 July Stauffenberg conspiracy. . . . Then he would tick off such things as the Rote Kapelle‡, which was the Communist espionage ring uncovered by the RSHA [Himmler's Secret Service]. . . .'

'But in that last fortnight when Hitler mentioned the leak, he knew what he was talking about – a steady flow of information out of the Bunker. For example he told me of an order a couple of months back, a routine promotion. Yet within forty-eight hours, he complained, the news of these promotions was on the British radio.'

So preoccupied was Hitler with this relatively unimportant leak that he told his personal pilot, Hans Baur, on the morning of the day he died, 'Baur, you can write on my tombstone, He *was betrayed by his generals*! 'Hitler wasn't, of course. There was a very simple explanation for the leak which concerned him so much during that last month of April 1945. As long as

---

* Like so many of the British Secret Service's high-ranking German captives, Berger never seemed to realize that his cell was bugged. Perhaps the captives thought the English wouldn't stoop so low!
‡ Red Orchestra.

the Bunker HQ used the Enigma coding machine then those slightly crazy Oxford dons far away in the English town of Bletchley would know as soon as Hitler's commanders what was going on beneath Berlin's bombed streets.

In their pride, however, the Führer's experts and Hitler himself could never believe that the technologically backward English would ever be able to penetrate the Enigma code.* Time and again, whenever the possibility was hesitantly raised, it was savaged by the German experts, just as they would never believe that the Anglo-Americans could be more advanced in the construction of an atomic bomb than their own scientists. But Germany was being betrayed by a spy at the very top. Even now in the intimate circle of these last-ditch Nazi survivors there was a spy transmitting their secrets to the enemy in London. So convinced was Hitler that he was being spied on all the time by the British that he would often remark sarcastically to his top-level advisers, Field Marshal Keitel and Colonel-General Jodl, 'I wonder if we can get this order off to the troops at the front before we hear about it over the London BBC.'

But for a couple of weeks now Hitler had not confined himself to paranoid outbreaks of rage and sarcastic remarks to his staff. He had insisted, somewhere in the first week of April 1945, that the matter of the leak should be urgently investigated. If the British, and perhaps their Russian allies too, knew what was going on in the underground Bunker, they might soon guess the great secret which he bore within him.

For by now Hitler had made his decision. He would never leave the Bunker. He had already revealed it in part to his long-time mistress Eva Braun, who had hitch-hiked, against his orders, from Berchtesgaden to be with him at the end.

---

* In an unusually light-hearted moment, Admiral Doenitz told the author that he had once thought that the Enigma code had been broken, but after a while he had dismissed the possibility, telling his Chief-of-Operations, 'The spy would have to be either you or me— and if it's not you, then it's me!'

Indeed, on that Monday 22 April 1945 she had scribbled her last note to her married sister Gretl Fegelein, wife of SS General Fegelein. It read: 'My dear little sister: Our end can come any minute. The Führer himself no longer believes a happy end is possible. You must take the necklace that the Führer gave me for my last birthday.'

Gretl Fegelein gratefully accepted the necklace in due course. After the war she was not inclined to comment on the fact that the man who had indirectly bestowed it upon her, Adolf Hitler, was the same who would have her husband shot in seven days' time. But by then that man was long dead.

Thus it was that Germany's most feared policemen were summoned to the doomed Bunker to discover the source of the leak which so agitated the Führer. Both were generals in the SS. One was nearly seven foot tall, a lawyer by profession, stupid and of frightening aspect. He was Dr Ernst Kaltenbrunner, an Austrian like the Führer, whose breath stank and whose scarface looked as if it had been carved out of wood by a drunken lumberjack with a blunt axe.

With him Kaltenbrunner had brought a real policeman, a man who had been a professional cop for a quarter of a century. His appearance, too, was slightly frightening, though his features did not immediately strike one as fearsome, at least compared to the giant who towered above him. His face was wooden, displaying no marked features. His skull seemed large, but it was that of his Bavarian peasant forefathers; there are many such to this day. The massive hands were in no way unusual either. Only his eyes seemed strange. As Captain Payne Best would describe them after the war; 'Funny eyes which he could flicker from side to side with the greatest rapidity'. Sitting on a turned-round chair, he would stare at his prisoner during an interrogation, occasionally leaning forward to bellow at the top of his voice in his thick Bavarian accent.

Not that he really needed to frighten his prisoners. His reputation always preceded him. As his subordinates invariably warned the victim-to-be, 'Achtung, jetzt kommt der Chef'. It took a strong-hearted man not to shudder. For they all knew who *der Chef* was: the most feared man in Europe, the head of the *Geheime Staatspolizei*, the Gestapo, which from 1940 to 1945 ruled with a rod of iron from Cracow to Calais and held 300 million Europeans under its sway. The man with the flickering eyes was SS General Heinrich Müller, known in that time of terror as 'Gestapo' Müller.

TWO

On the same day that it was decided to issue the codeword 'Clausewitz', Germany's central bank in the surrounded capital, the *Reichsbank* was raided for the last time. But this particular raid was not the work of the 'Anglo-American aerial terrorists', who had already bombed the bank several times. Now the raid came from below and was carried out by Germans, the SS to be exact.

On the orders of General Kaltenbrunner, a group of heavily armed SS men under the command of 39-year-old SS *Brigadeführer* Josef Spacil, head of the Black Guards' Budget Administration Section, burst into the bank, weapons at the ready. At pistol point they herded the frightened clerks, tellers and the like down to the vaults. Here the SS forced them to remove jewels, securities and Germany's last remaining foreign exchange assets to the tune of 23 million gold marks (approximately ten million dollars in those days).

Hurriedly, almost all that was left of Germany's wealth was transported out of the ruined city. The Russians were bombarding the dying capital again and the roads south had already been cut. But Spacil managed to guide his party through the various dangers. Within hours, most of the loot was on its way south by plane. Behind a triumphant Spacil and his precious haul he left a Berlin in flames. The *Brigadeführer* must have breathed a sigh of relief. He was heading for the high mountains of the Tyrol. Just as his master had ordered him. Most of the loot would be hidden till the day

19

came for a new Reich to claim it. But there was still plenty left for his own use and that of his boss, Kaltenbrunner, and his mistress, *Gräfin* Westrop, who had already fled to the area and was waiting impatiently for her giant lover, and her share of the loot.

The great bank robbery, carried out by the 'most loyal of the loyal', Hitler's SS, was significant. It showed the way that Kaltenbrunner and the rest of the top SS brass were thinking. For weeks now Kaltenbrunner had been handing out forged new papers to certain key members of his staff who wished to become 'U-boats and take a dive', as the usage of the time had it. One of those subordinates had been Colonel Eichmann. The latter had refused, flourishing his pistol and maintaining that that was the way out he would take. All the same, Kaltenbrunner and his colleague Colonel Hoettl noted cynically that the scourge of Europe's Jews had organized his own private *Fuchsbau** in Berlin.

As Hoettl wrote after the war: 'When the Gestapo Headquarters in the Prinz Albrecht Strasse had been destroyed by bombs, Eichmann set up his Berlin office in the Kurfuersten Strasse. When air-raid shelters were being constructed beneath his new offices, he took the opportunity of organizing what he called his "foxes' lair". Underground rooms were built and stocked with food, water, medicine and first-aid appliances. Lighting and plumbing were installed for a long stay. These shelters were not built directly under the offices but some way off and were connected to them by a labyrinth of passages. . . . The exits and air shafts debouching into various bomb-damaged sites were camouflaged to harmonize with their surroundings.'

Kaltenbrunner thought little of his fellow Austrian Eichmann's† plan to go to ground in Berlin. He thought it too dangerous. He would have to rely on too many people who might betray him and he knew what *his* fate would be if he fell into the hands of the Russians. No, he would escape to the

* Foxes' lair.
† Eichmann had been born in Germany, but had spent most of his early life in Austria and spoke German with an Austrian accent.

20

freer air of his native land, where, in an emergency, he could walk across the mountain frontier into Italy and disappear and where he had many friends and comrades who would rather die than betray him.

In the event Kaltenbrunner would be betrayed in Austria by the one person he should have been able to trust, his mistress. But on that Monday, when he attended the Bunker for the last time with Müller, that possibility had not occurred to him, nor the fact that he and all those like him were not safe anyway. Just like his chief Himmler, Kaltenbrunner had not realized the enormity of the crimes they had carried out in Germany's name. The whole of the Western World demanded punishment and retribution. There was nowhere for them to hide.

As he said his goodbye and handed over the case to Müller, Kaltenbrunner must have wondered what plans for the future were going through the Bavarian peasant's head. Müller, he knew, had served the old Bavarian monarchy, the Weimar Government *and* the Third Reich. He was no fanatical Nazi (as we shall see, he was indeed the absolute contrary). He was a survivor. But how was he to survive? Kaltenbrunner didn't know. For, as always, Müller played the power game with his cards close to his chest.

So he left, leaving behind Müller, now the senior police-man in Germany, still on active duty, surrounded by men he had known for nearly a quarter of a century, nearly all of whom hated and feared him. Had he not once persecuted the older ones among them before they came into power in 1933? He had even told his cronies prior to that date that the Führer was 'a no-good Austrian draft-dodger and un-employed house-painter', whom he'd 'take care of in due course'.

That Monday Müller must have sensed the animosity of the *Parteiprominenz* still left in the Bunker. But if he did, he gave no sign of it. He was on a case, one of the kind he liked best. Ever since 1933 it had been his lot to tackle such cases involving Party shots – ones dealing with treachery, betrayal, sexual perversions, murder and, best of all, espionage.

It was he who had solved the mystery of British

Intelligence's assassination of his former boss, Reinhard Heydrich[*]. It was he who had broken the 'Red Orchestra', that all-embracing Russian spy organization which had reached to the very top in Party and aristocratic circles in Berlin. The downfall of Admiral Canaris' *Abwehr* (Military Intelligence) network had been partly his work. Espionage cases were right up his street, even now at this eleventh hour.

Systematic as always, Müller now set about finding the person who was allegedly leaking the information from the doomed Bunker. Naturally he used the professional policeman's traditional approach: motive, opportunity, means, etc. Right from the start it was clear that if anyone was really leaking information to the British of the kind broadcast over the BBC, which was not only military but also personal, it had to be someone at the top. That someone had to be a person with the ability to leave the Bunker and hand what he had found out to a second person. For all wireless communications leaving the underground shelter were monitored and recorded; and so far nothing of a suspicious nature had been noted by the listeners.

So who could leave the Bunker, *and return*, without too much difficulty? Who had the means of getting through the encircling Russians without endangering themselves; in other words, who had the use of armoured vehicles, even possibly a light aircraft, such as a Fieseler Storch, which could land and take off on the streets not far from the Bunker?

Müller soon had a short list of suspects who knew the Führer's movements within the Bunker and might have the opportunity to pass in and out of the place. There was SS General Rattenhuber, head of the Leader's bodyguard. He fitted all categories save one: he'd be missed immediately if he ventured out even for a short period. In a way, just like the man he watched over, he was under constant supervision. Rattenhuber could be scratched off the list.

[*] See C. Whiting: *Heydrich* and *Hitler's Dirty War* (both Pen & Sword) for further details.

There was the 'Duke of Swabia', SS General Berger, the founder of the *Waffen SS*. He was a likely choice. The flamboyant General changed sides as often as he did his shirt and he had opportunity enough to leave the Bunker on some liaison mission or other. But Müller rejected him too. Berger would not want to take the slightest risk at this stage of the war. He was passionately devoted to saving his own skin and spying was a dangerous business.

As for the other liaison officers who left the Bunker every day to contact Army and SS headquarters outside Berlin or in the suburbs, their numbers were drying up rapidly. Since 'Clausewitz' there was little need for their services. All main headquarters were moving to the far south or the north-west. Daily contacts with those far-off headquarters were about to come to an end.

It was now that Müller had a brainwave, though it could hardly be called that. He was not given to spontaneous flights of inspired guesswork. His conclusions were invariably based on stolid plodding and, when he had a prisoner to help him along, the use of his fists and application of his *Gummiknueppel*, his rubber club. What if the culprit was still posing as a liaison officer, although the headquarters to which he was assigned outside the Bunker had already moved? Instead of visiting the rear echelon of this HQ, where there remained no principals to give him the information he needed for the Führer (not that the Führer was any longer in a fit state to absorb any information), was he visiting someone else close by?

Up until recently, as was customary in Germany*, the *Einwohnermeldeamt* (Resident's Registry Office) recorded the address and details of every person living in Berlin. Within seconds the police could find out who lived where and with whom. It was illegal not to have these details registered within one week of moving to a new address, even if it was just across the road from one's old address. But since the Russians had surrounded Berlin and the chaotic state of

---

* And it still is today.

the city administration due to bombing and the shelling, that had all gone by the board. People lived 'wild', as the saying went. Even Müller did, with his mistress and illegitimate children. No one in authority knew where people were this April.

Having come to that conclusion, Müller now started to cast around for one of the remaining liaison officers of sufficient rank and authority to obtain top-level information and who still left the Bunker to 'liaise', presumably, with the agent of the power he was spying for. Müller, who had supposedly been fighting the intelligence agents of both Soviet Russia and Britain for most of the last five years, could guess which power it was – England! Everyone knew that the English were the most cunning spies of them all. Germany had nothing to match them.

It was now that chance played into Müller's hands and, in due course, delivered the 'spy', if that was what he really was, as if on a silver platter. On Wednesday, 25 April, two days after the 'Clausewitz' signal had been flashed across Berlin, SS General Fegelein, of whom we have already heard and who was married to Eva Braun's sister, Gretl, left the Bunker. He said he was going to visit Himmler's HQ at Hohenlychen. In the mass hysteria and drunkenness which was beginning to afflict most of the inmates of the Bunker, no one took much notice of his departure for the *Reichsführer* SS's headquarters. As far as is known, not one of the high-ranking officers who surrounded Hitler queried the journey. They should have, of course. Hitler had left them in no doubt that in his view the SS had let him down and there were ugly rumours circulating in the Bunker that Himmler was already having secret talks with the Allies in an attempt to save his own skin and ensure some kind of position for himself in a defeated post-war Germany. As he himself had expressed it to his cronies, 'Give me five minutes with Eisenhower and I am sure I can convince him we can talk man to man.' It was to be a pious hope. Himmler would be dead by his own hand before that terrible spring was over.

On the late evening of that same Wednesday, Fegelein returned to Berlin by air. But he didn't go back to the Bunker.

In retrospect, one wonders why he undertook the hazardous return flight in the first place. He had already told his fellow SS generals at Hohenlychen that he had no intention of dying in the Bunker. He had sneered to SS General Max Juettner that he'd have no part in the mass suicide planned for the Bunker dwellers: 'The Valhalla stuff is for the Bayreuth Festival, but not for me. Goebbels is even sounding off about an SS plan to blow the Bunker complex sky-high with TNT. The place has become a lunatic asylum.' So why did he return? We don't really know, and if Müller, in due course, found out, he disappeared without telling anyone.

So Fegelein didn't return to the Bunker. Nor did he on the following day, and it was only on the third day, Friday April 27, that his absence was noted. According to the handful of survivors, it was Hitler himself who asked where Fegelein was. Why the Führer should have been interested in the lowly SS cavalry general when his world was falling apart can only be explained by the fact that within three days Fegelein would become his brother-in-law.

Now it was discovered, under Hitler's prompting, that Fegelein had missed six of the last briefings. The Führer's rage flared up. He demanded to know what Fegelein was up to and where he was. To all present, it came as a shock to learn that he had no contact number or address *outside* the Bunker. 'Where in the devil's name *is* he?' Hitler demanded. In the end he called General Rattenhuber, head of the bodyguard and, like Müller, an ex-cop from Bavaria. The latter received a severe dressing-down from the Führer, who at times was spitting with rage. Shaken, the head of the bodyguard bumped into SS Major Guensche, an old drinking companion of the missing General and another future brother-in-law.

Guensche now revealed that he had a secret telephone number for Fegelein. The number was that of a modest flat in unbombed Bleibetreustrasse (the not very aptly named secret hideaway)* and Fegelein answered Rattenhuber's call personally. He was shocked when he heard Rattenhuber's

* In German it means 'Stay true'.

voice, but recovered quickly, saying he had a terrible hangover from the previous night's boozing session and was unshaven. Rattenhuber ordered him to shave immediately and report for duty. Fegelein gave him his word of honour as a German officer that he'd be at the Bunker within two hours. But it appears that he and his mysterious foreign lady companion had other plans. Two hours passed and still he had not made an appearance, shaven or otherwise. Instead he called Eva Braun, who apparently knew Fegelein was going to do a bunk. Now he brazenly announced that he was going to take a dive and, if she liked, he would take her with him. How and to where is not recorded. It is recorded, however, that Eva grew indignant and reminded him that Gretl was in Bavaria and due to have a baby at any moment. That cut no ice with Fegelein, who had probably, in his mind, already abandoned his wife of only a year. If Hitler committed suicide now, what good would the Eva Braun–Gretl connection be? However, if that was case, and that was the way Fegelein was thinking, why had he suggested taking Eva with him into the unknown? And why was he risking his life in Berlin when he could have fled westwards from Hohenlychen long ago?

But the time was not ripe for such questions inside the Bunker. Indeed time was running out fast for Hitler and his followers. At five that afternoon, when Fegelein had still not appeared as promised, a young SS officer was sent to the Berlin apartment to bring Fegelein in. But when he arrived he found Fegelein drunk once again. He tried to convince him to return with him, but the General refused and asked the young officer to desert with him. Presumably Fegelein thought this would delay any further attempt to reach him before whatever he was waiting for appeared.

Indignantly the SS officer, Captain Frick, refused, as he also refused Fegelein's offer of some cognac. Instead he set off on the dangerous journey back to the Bunker. As a junior captain, naturally he couldn't arrest an SS General. Someone higher in rank than he would have to take on that unpleasant task.

Halfway back to the Bunker Frick's luck ran out. He was

spotted by a Russian forward artillery observer who brought down a barrage of shells on the lone vehicle. It was hit, as was Frick, in both arm and leg. Some time later the vehicle, both front tyres shot to ribbons, limped into the debris-littered courtyard of the Reich Chancellery. Frick staggered out to report, but he didn't get far.

It was about that time that the most powerful man in Germany, still the power behind the throne, 'the Brown Eminence' as he has been called*, got into the act. Martin Bormann, Hitler's Secretary since 1941, listened to Frick's report carefully, but with growing impatience. Then he flared up, directing his rage at the unfortunate Rattenhuber, demanding to know why he had sent such a low-ranking officer as Frick to deal with an SS General.

An embarrassed Rattenhuber, who had already felt the lash of Hitler's tongue that day, had no answer for the *Reichsleiter*. After a long and fairly heated discussion, it was decided to send another party to Fegelein, commanded by Rattenhuber's second-in-command, Colonel Hoegl. Frick, whose wounds had been now tended, would guide them, though he wondered why Rattenhuber was not going with them. Colonel Hoegl didn't have the rank to arrest General Fegelein either, if that was their intention, while Rattenhuber did. But the head of Hitler's bodyguard was too much of an old hand to want to risk his own skin at this stage of the game. Hoegl would have to suffice.

But what was Hoegl supposed to do? Attempt to arrest Fegelein, or simply bring him back to the Bunker?

And why was Fegelein still waiting in that modest apartment at Number Ten, Bleibetreustrasse? Surely Captain Frick's visit should have warned him? Sooner or later the Führer's minions were bound to make a second attempt and this time it could well be by force. And who was the woman Frick had spotted in the back of the apartment? Once Eva Braun learned, as she surely would, that he was betraying her beloved, pregnant sister with another woman, he could

---

* Brown because he wore the brown uniform of the Party.

expect no help from that important quarter. Why didn't he make a run for it while there was still time? After all, he had told General Juettner two days before that he wasn't to go down with the sinking ship.

A lot of questions, with few answers.

THREE

In June, 1944, the month in which the Western Allies landed in Normandy, Hitler had given a frugal dinner at his house in Obersalzberg for General Fegelein and his new bride, Eva's sister Gretl Braun. It had consisted of a thin pea soup, followed by meat for them and a vegetarian dish for himself, one glass of champagne, a cup of peppermint tea for the Führer and, as a treat, a slice of *Sahnetorte*, which Hitler dearly loved.

But this had not been sufficient for Eva. She complained that, due to her liaison with Hitler, she was never allowed to attend any real festive occasion. She wanted a big party in the German fashion for her sister and, naturally, herself.

Just as Bormann had selected the expensive diamond tiara for the bride's wedding present, now he arranged a big party as soon as the Führer had left for his HQ. As charming and polite as he could be to his private guests, Hitler was a bit of a bore; his presence always awed and subdued his guests, who felt that they had to watch what they drank, ate and said.

The wedding party was a smashing success. It lasted for days and moved from Bormann's house on the 'Mountain', as the area of Hitler's private holiday home was called, to the Teahouse, which Bormann had 'given' to the Führer on his 50th birthday, and on to other houses down near Berchtesgaden below. The locals, who were now barred from the 'Mountain' where they had once grazed their cattle in the summer months, said that the guests had been drunk from morning to night.

29

In the end Bormann suggested to Fegelein that they should drink *Bruederschaft*. This ceremony, which meant being able to call one another by their first names, was a great honour in the typically formal German society of the time. Fegelein was flattered; not many men called the 'Brown Eminence' Martin. So their glasses were filled, their arms interlocked, they raised their glasses, cried, *'Ex'*, drained their glasses and said 'Martin' and 'Otto'. Now they were supposedly bosom friends for life. But were they?

Now, a year later, Bormann flew into a blinding rage with his erstwhile *'Duzfreund'* (literally 'thou-friend', someone with whom he was on first-name terms). The Führer had calmed down, having realized that Fegelein's absence was not all that important in the light of the overall situation. But not Bormann.

Hoegl had returned from Fegelein's flat to explain what had transpired. He'd found the General with an unknown woman, washed and shaved, but obviously not intending to return to the Bunker. Instead he was helping the woman to pack a valise – and he was drunk again.

Indeed the first thing Fegelein did was to offer the SS Colonel a drink and, seemingly going to fetch the drinks, the woman disappeared with a tray of empty glasses into the kitchen. Hoegl could hear water being run and assumed she was washing the glasses up before replenishing them.

Naturally it was all a trick. Fegelein kept Hoegl occupied while the woman slipped out of the kitchen window never to be seen again. Now an unhappy Colonel Hoegl returned with the drunken General to be confronted, not only by Rattenhuber and Major Guensche, but also by Bormann and Müller.

Bormann didn't wait for lengthy explanations. He emptied the contents of the woman's valise on to a table and Hoegl gasped when he saw what they were: diamonds, gold watches (including one Eva Braun had given her brother-in law to have repaired for her), a hundred thousand Reichsmarks and 3,186 Swiss francs. There were also road maps and two different passports bearing the same picture but separate names. And one of those passports bore the seal of the United Kingdom! It was a British passport. It seemed that Fegelein, like many others, was going to make a run for it, *with a foreign woman!*

Bormann roared at Hoegl, 'You flat-footed idiot! Where's the woman? Why didn't you grab her and bring her back instead of this damned valise? Fegelein is a traitor. This woman is British, an enemy agent. Fegelein went to bed with her and blabbed everything. *She was the leak.'*

It was an interesting outburst. Why should Bormann have been so enraged? As soon as the time was ripe he too was going to flee the Bunker. He had already warned his wife to leave the 'Mountain' and head for the Italian Bolzano area with the children. There he would join her in due course. Why should Bormann be so agitated by Fegelein for seemingly taking the same escape route?

Was it the fact that Fegelein's mistress might have been English and, therefore, supposedly a spy that aroused his anger? But as Dr Schenk, the SS doctor who volunteered to stay and tend the wounded in the Bunker, has testified, there were all sorts of nationalities in the Bunker itself, including one Englishman. * As Schenk related long afterwards, one of the wounded officers he tended in the makeshift Bunker hospital amazed him by saying, 'I am an Englishman by birth. My name is Engels. I am a grandson of Friedrich Engels, the friend of Karl Marx.' It was only years later that Dr Schenk realized the full significance of the wounded officer's statement. He was not only an Englishman, but also the descendant of the socialist friend of the founder of communism and both were Jews!

Why, then, was Bormann so concerned about this unknown woman, who might or might not have been part of that leak which had originally agitated Hitler so much? Was there more to it than Hoegl and Rattenhuber suspected? Why did Müller allow himself to be roped in when he, too, was about to

---

* There is also the interesting case of Else Kruger, Bormann's 29-year-old secretary, one of the last to see him alive in the Bunker before he fled. Two years after fleeing the Bunker herself, she turned up in, of all places, one of Britain's ancient universities!

depart? Again a lot of questions without apparent answers. But one thing did become clear in those last hours Bormann and Müller spent together in the Bunker. It is this. Although they were superficially comrades and drinking cronies, neither liked the other; yet Müller spent his last recorded hours dealing with this, for him, unimportant matter of the disgraced SS General Otto Fegelein.

Now things moved fast. It was discovered that the woman, who was seemingly an Englishwoman married to an Hungarian diplomat in Berlin*, worked as a linguist in Berlin radio's *Deutschlandsender*. Guensche and Hitler's pilot, Hans Bauer, had both met her. In her thirties, she was tall and well-groomed. Both thought that her husband had been arrested at the time that Germany and Hungary broke off diplomatic relations in late 1944, that after her husband had been taken away she had taken up with Fegelein, whose wife was far away in Bavaria. Whether she used him merely as a protector or an informant at the highest level Bauer and Guensche couldn't say.

Bormann, who had been in charge of the investigation into the leak before Müller was called in, obviously thought the latter. For now he ordered that the woman be arrested and the flat checked out more thoroughly. Two parties then set off, one under Rattenhuber, the other under Müller. Taking different routes through Berlin's bombed and burning streets, they arrived within five minutes of each other to find, naturally, that the bird had flown.

Fegelein was handed over to Müller's Gestapo subordinates and Müller proceeded directly from the flat to the cellar used by the Gestapo interrogators under the nearby *Dreifaltigkeit* (Trinity) Chapel. Here Fegelein remained, probably being questioned about the woman, for all of Saturday. It is doubtful that Müller personally would have used torture. He was well known for his rigorous, sometimes illegal, methods of interrogation, but he had never been known to use torture. Besides, it seems obvious that he was

---

* Hungary had been Germany's ally for over two years.

glad to be away from the Bunker and Fegelein's interrogation provided a legitimate excuse.

According to most reports Fegelein was never seen again by any of the Bunker *Prominenz*. All the same, his fate was not sealed until about nine o'clock that Saturday night. Seven thousand miles away at the San Francisco Conference, British Foreign Secretary Anthony Eden inadvertently let slip that Himmler was suing for peace via the neutral Swedes, led by the King of Sweden's cousin Count Folke Bernadotte. An alert Reuter's man picked up the news, managed to get it through the censorship and his scoop was subsequently broadcast to the world. In due course it was picked up by the German DNB man in the Bunker and passed on to Hitler.

The news exploded like a bombshell. Himmler a traitor! Hitler was shattered by the news. His 'loyal Heinrich', as the Führer called him, had betrayed him. It was the end. Wild stories flourished. The SS was going to raid the Bunker. The Führer's body was going to be handed over to the Russians. No, it was to be given to Eisenhower as a pledge that Himmler was serious. Now everyone connected with Himmler was suspect.

Hitler, who, as we have seen, was to marry Fegelein's sister-in-law before he departed this world, no longer felt he could protect the guilty man. So far he had simply had Fegelein stripped of his rank and Knight's Cross. Now he ordered his death.

Eva Braun made no attempt to plead for her brother-in-law. Besides, Hitler was determined to marry his mistress of fifteen years before he died, and that was something that made Eva forget all other considerations, even her own impending death.

She was a silly woman, despite her thirty-three years and the decade and a half she had spent at Hitler's side. As a child she had tried to win her father's love by excelling at sport, disdaining girlish interests. Then she had taken a Jewish boyfriend, liked to imitate the Jewish singer Al Jolson and dreamed of becoming a film star. Thereafter she had been Hitler's backstreet mistress, always kept out of sight and consoling herself with French underwear, champagne and bright lipsticks.

So while Eva prepared for the great event, Fegelein was taken out by Müller and his assistants and presumably shot. No body was ever found, nor even a grave. Fegelein simply disappeared, as did so many of them in the Bunker that last night. An hour after Fegelein's death Hitler married Eva. As Gerda Christian, Hitler's secretary, reported after the war: 'There were tears in her blue eyes.' But they weren't for the newly dead Fegelein. 'They were tears of radiant joy.' Fegelein had already been forgotten.

Now Eva Hitler showed off the wedding ring given to her by the Führer and told the women clustered around her, 'You can safely call me Mrs Hitler now.'

But Mrs Hitler's new-found happiness was not to last long. She knew now that she was going to die, and soon. After the initial euphoria had passed, she summoned her long-time help, Liesl Ostertag. She told her that she wanted Liesl to accept two of her most precious possessions. These were the silk nightie she had worn on her wedding night with Hitler and the new wedding ring. Liesl should hide them carefully and when the time was opportune should take them southwards and give them to Eva's best friend, her beloved Herta. Liesl agreed and disappeared to become a minor footnote in the history of the Second World War.

Hitler and his new wife then committed suicide and the surviving rats began to leave the sinking ship. Over the years Hitler had often pondered aloud among his cronies where he would be buried. In one will, filed in 1938, he had expressed the wish that 'upon my death, my remains should be transported to Munich. . . . They shall be properly displayed on a catafalque before the *Feldherrnhalle* *. . . . After the state funeral, which is to be solemn yet simple, my body is to be removed to the Temple of National Socialism on the *Königsplatz* [also in Munich]. There I shall rest under the eternal flame.'

Hitler was never to return to Munich, but many of those now

---

* The site of the place where Hitler's 'Munich Putsch' took place and of his first abortive bid for power.

slinking out of the Bunker returned to the scene of the original crime. Some would not enjoy their freedom for long. Sooner or later there would come that discreet knock on the door which they had been expecting. They'd rush to the back door, straight into the arms of the waiting CIC agent. A few of the least important would get away with it and disappear for good and, as they were mostly small fry first the Americans and then the Federal Germans would give up on them and let them run.

But here and there there were a handful of men present in the Bunker that April of 1945 who would be sought by the authorities, both American and German and, in the end, those of the rest of the free world, decades later, men who would now be over a hundred years old, still on the official wanted lists. One of these was Gestapo Müller. Where had *he* gone?

1923: DATE WITH DESTINY

'If that should be the case, or I should die, it would only be a sign that my star has run its course and my mission is fulfilled.'

Adolf Hitler, 9 November 1923

ONE

On 7 November 1918 a revolution broke out in Munich. It was led by a small, elderly Jew, Kurt Eisner, a German and ultra-left-wing socialist. With his black, floppy hat, his cloak and shock of dark hair, he looked like the caricature of an anarchist, with a large round object held in his hand labelled 'bomb'. Surprisingly enough the caricature knew his business – to a degree. By evening his 'revolutionaries', mostly war-weary socialists and workers, together with a large number of dissatisfied soldiers, had thrown out the Wittelsbach monarchy and seized the main Bavarian government buildings. Next morning the burghers of Munich woke up to find that they now lived in a republic. It had all been done in typically German style, without too much fuss and with not a single casualty. Lenin had mocked that there could never be a revolution in Germany because the people wouldn't dare to walk on the grass if it were *verboten*. The Soviet dictator had been proved wrong, though another Jewish leader of the new revolution, Ernst Toller, did telegraph Moscow to inform Lenin, apropos of nothing, that the key to the lavatory of the Foreign Ministry was missing; what should he do? Lenin did not deign to reply.

Farce was soon to turn into tragedy, however. Older burghers would long remember '*die Roten*' and '*die Juden*', who made a battlefield of their city, which, in certain areas, turned into a bloodbath. The first to feel the backlash was Eisner himself. It was whispered that he was being financed by Russian communist gold. He wasn't. His revolution that November day had cost him exactly eighteen marks, paid out of his own pocket. No matter. Deciding to resign, he was assassinated by a right-wing 19-year-old cavalry officer, Count Arco-Valley. It didn't matter that Arco-Valley was half-Jewish himself. He became a hero of the extreme right and a hated enemy of the extreme left.

Martial law was declared, a general strike was called and the situation began to escalate. Armed civilians – they even had heavy machine guns and cannon – appeared on the streets, men in uniform too, though they had torn off their rank epaulettes and unit identification so it was unclear whether they were members of the communist workers-and-soldiers' councils or of the right-wing Free Corps, now apparently marching on Munich to put down the 'Red Revolution'.

Munich was in for a battle and it got it. The right staged a putsch which was put down by communist forces within the city. They were led by Eugene Levin, not only a Jew, but a virulent communist and a Russian to boot'.

It was a combination that must have delighted the right-wing insurgents as it played right into the hands of their propagandists.* Native Germans, more importantly native Bavarians, were being enslaved by one of Moscow's Jewish Bolsheviks! Now an army, some 8,000 strong, marched to Dachau, some eight miles from the Bavarian capital. Here it halted and prepared for an attack on the city's communist rulers. What were the revolutionaries going to do?

The Munich communists released a fellow revolutionary whom they had just jailed as some kind of deviationist. He was the playwright Ernst Toller, the man who had cabled Lenin about the key to the Bavarian Foreign Ministry's lavatory. He had been Eisner's chief-of-staff and was supposed to know something about military matters. He didn't, of course, but in that crazy time, what did it matter?

---

* In fact the anti-communist forces were under the command of the exiled Social Democratic government of one Hoffmann. But Hoffmann's actual armed fighting force was mostly composed of right-wingers and nationalist Bavarians.

Toller was ordered to stop the counter-revolutionaries at Dachau and he didn't hesitate. Commandeering a horse and declaring that a 'revolution must be fought cleanly', he set off to meet the enemy.

On 18 April 1919 he reached the place that remains infamous to this day, Dachau. Here he tried to negotiate with the opposition. From Munich they urged him to use his artillery. At first he refused, but in the end he was forced to fire his handful of cannon on the counter-revolutionaries, who panicked and fled, leaving many of their officers prisoner.

Munich's Central Committee, taking a leaf out of Moscow's book, ordered them shot out of hand. Toller, in a supposedly noble gesture, refused. The Central Committee's reaction was predictable. The Commander-in-Chief was arrested once more and put back in prison.

Now another breed of German entered the battle. Noske, the Socialist War Minister in Berlin, ordered one of the right-wing Free Corps working with the hated socialists, the men who had 'stabbed them in the back', as they often proclaimed, into battle.* The 'Sow Prussians' (*Saupreuss*), as the Bavarians always called their traditional enemies, were on their way.†

Frightened out of their wits, the Munich Reds savagely hunted down their enemies, supposed and real, still inside the city. Hostages were taken and threatened with summary execution if the Free Corps didn't stop its advance. Again Toller was released to act as Commander-in-Chief of the 'Red Army'. This time the fight was no joke. The Free Corps shot a dozen unarmed workers and fifty-two Russian POWs. At the time a certain Corporal Hitler was on a supposed cushy number guarding Russian prisoners-of-war, of whom there were still many in Bavaria.

---

* While they had been fighting at the front, the Jews and socialists back home had sold them out to their enemies, the Western Allies. Thus they were 'stabbed in the back'.
† Even to this day in the German border dialects of Luxembourg, Belgium and Lorraine the Germans are known as 'Prussians', reflecting the folk memory of the Prussian invaders of the mid-19th century.

41

The Reds retaliated. Twenty of the hundred hostages kept in the well-known Luitpold High School were 'liquidated'. The civil war escalated. On 1 May 1919 the workers celebrated 'May Day' while the Free Corps toughs started to enter Munich from several directions. Opposition was light as most people were glad to see them. It would bring an end to the fighting and, for many, starvation. Food in the city, cut off from its rural supplies, could only be obtained on the black market at exorbitant prices.

The main station was soon taken. Schwabing, Munich's artist quarter where Toller had held away the year before, followed. The Free Corps men, Prussians though they might be, were the heroes of the hour. In the Marienplatz, near the twin-towered central church, an open-air mass was held. Ceremonially the red flag of revolution was tugged down and in its place the blue-and-white chequered flag of the *Freistaat Bayern* was raised.

Far away in Moscow the Soviet dictator Lenin boasted of a 'spontaneous' mass demonstration in Red Square proving that communism was triumphant everywhere. 'The liberated working class is celebrating its anniversary [May Day] freely and openly, not only in Soviet Russia, but in Soviet Hungary and Soviet Bavaria.' In reality murder squads from the North German Free Corps sent by Noske, a fellow socialist, were cruising the streets of Munich hunting out 'Reds, Jews and *franc-tireurs*'. Their method was simple and not very foolproof. A glance at the suspect's hands and down with his trousers. If there were powder burns and he was circumcized he was a 'Red sniper'. Summary justice followed instantly. By the end of that May Day fatalities were into their hundreds. Two days later a thousand dead bodies littered the city. The next day the City Council had returned to form. They were worried now, not by 'bloody revolution', but by the decaying bodies. The city, they thought, looked 'very untidy'.

Munich had experienced its only revolution since that of 1848. It had been dealt with cruelly but swiftly. There was, however, a price to be paid in the new republic for having averted a revolution *à la Russe*. The fact that Eisner's attempt to take over the Bavarian state after the flight of the

Wittelsbach monarchy had been carried out by Jews and communists gave rise to dozens of semi-secret right-wing societies. These were in the main vehemently anti-communist and anti-semitic. They ranged from the mystic Thule Society, which had intellectual pretensions and pioneered the swastika symbol, to the 'German Workers' Party', set up by an obscure railway fitter called Anton Drexler.

'Once the handsome and comfortable city attracted the best minds of the Reich,' Jewish novelist Leon Feuchtwanger wrote of Munich later. 'How did it happen that they were now gone and that in their place everything that was rotten and unable to maintain itself elsewhere was magically pulled towards Munich?'

Be that as it may, the man who was to fuse all these various elements and sects together, however crackpot, was already in place. In Munich that year was a skinny, yellow-faced Army corporal with an old-fashioned 'tea-strainer' moustache, who was soon to be demobilized from the beaten ex-Imperial Army and was wondering what he should do next. The victors were already planning to limit the future German army to 100,000 regular soldiers and there'd be no place for him in it. He had not made much of a success of his immediate post-war career since his release from a military hospital. He had guarded Russian POWs and had kept his head down during the recent revolution. Indeed, the only gainful employment he had undertaken in this period was not something one talked about openly in Munich that year. He had spied on those in his Bavarian Infantry Regiment who had sided with the 'Reds', and most of his comrades had seemingly been so inclined.

The yellow-faced corporal was of course Adolf Hitler. Soon he would be demobbed to an uncertain future. Till that time Army Intelligence used him to lecture his fellow soldiers, also about to be released, on the evil of communism and the political dangers awaiting them in the civilian world. A loner even in the forced cameraderie of the wartime frontline trenches, Hitler developed rapidly. He discovered an unsuspected talent for public speaking and he didn't need much instruction on what exactly were the dangers awaiting these military innocents in wicked Munich. He knew them already.

43

'We have not bled for workers and for red councils,' he declared fervently. 'Where are the thanks of our Fatherland? . . . The Jews are a racial tuberculosis. . . . They must be deliberately removed. . . . All Jews deserve to be hanged. They are guilty of war.'*

In the autumn of 1919 he was invited to join one of the tiny political parties he was supposed to be keeping tabs on – Drexler's German Workers' Party. He had, for better or worse, entered the Munich political arena.

That summer another corporal who had won the Iron Cross at the front, just as Hitler had in 1918, also started out on his career, also in Munich. But his place of work was not in one of the seedy eating places such as the *Fürstenfelder Hof* or *Sterneckerbrau* favoured by the would-be political leader. Instead, this 19-year-old corporal, just back from France, began where he would end his 26-year-long career – in a police headquarters. A native Bavarian, with a broad Munich accent which he never tried to lose, he started his career in Munich's impressive *Polizeipräsidium*. Not that he was anyone of importance. He was to start on the lowest rung of the ladder, a lowly, poorly paid clerk with the title (everyone in Germany had to have a title in a country where even the wife of a humble chimneysweep will call herself, '*Frau Schornsteinfeger*', Mrs Chimneysweep) of 'auxiliary assistant'. One couldn't get lower.

But even that was better than the alternative – to become one of the ever-growing army of half-starved unemployed, its ranks swollen daily by thousands of recently demobilized servicemen. For Müller had the average German working-class man's fear of being unemployed – *stempelngehen*, literally 'to go stamping'. Being unemployed was not just a misfortune to such people, it was a crime.

Müller had been born into a traditional Catholic Bavarian working-class family in the decent working-class suburb of Munich-Pasing. His parents were of a type common then.

* Later in life Hitler declared that it was in that year he discovered that 'I could speak. In the course of my lectures I led many hundreds, indeed thousands, of comrades back to their people and Fatherland.'

44

They were proud of being Bavarian; they hated the 'Prussians', meaning all North Germans; they were strict churchgoers, but they also loved the easy life-style of Munich with its beer-gardens and one-litre stone mugs of good Bavarian beer, which at weekends they consumed in vast quantities, both men, women and, it must be said, children too. They seem to have been born with the command on their lips, *'Noch a' Mass'* – another measure, waiter.

Müller passed all eight classes of his *Volksschule* without once getting the blue letter.* In the same year the war broke out and the Bavarian Army under Prince Rupprecht marched to the front, Heinrich marched off to start his three-year apprenticeship, as was expected of all decent Bavarian working-class children. His parents obtained an apprenticeship for him as a metal fitter in one of the capital's industries of the future, as we would say today, in the Bavarian Aircraft Engine Works.

In 1917, his apprenticeship finished and with another year to go before he would be called up for military service, which he probably would not have been anyway, due to his job, Müller did something uncharacteristic. For already many of the workers, after three years of fighting, no longer supported the war with same unquestioning loyalty they had shown in August 1914. He volunteered for military service, in particular for the air branch of the *Heer*.

Even more surprisingly, at a time when few pilots came from the working classes – all the German aces seemed to come from well-born or aristocratic families – Müller was accepted for pilot training and duly qualified. His career was not particularly outstanding, but he was promoted to corporal and in due course he had the Iron Cross, first and second class, before he was demobilized in July 1919.

He was fortunate to find the low-paid assistant's job in the Police Ministry. Naturally his record spoke for him. He was a Bavarian Nationalist who had joined the recently formed

* A letter in this colour, telling the parents their child had not achieved the class target for that year and would have to remain behind (*sitzenbleiben*) to take the year again. This was regarded as a terrible shame on the family.

45

(1918) Bavarian People's Party; he had a good war record and he was already courting the daughter of the Party's main paper's owner. He was, on the surface at least, a regular churchgoer and the Catholic Church exerted an important influence in Munich. In other words he had, as the Germans put it, 'the right Party book'.

All the same, he knew that post-war Germany, and in particular Bavaria, was racked by dissatisfaction and impending starvation. He might have the right party book in 1919, but what of 1920? As a police official of the Bavarian State Ministry of the Interior wrote that winter, 'movements are without doubt dangerous to the government, not only for the present form of government but for any political system, because if they really achieve their dark ideas in regard to the Jews, Social Democrats and Bank-capitalists, then there will be much blood and disorder.'

Müller was not particularly worried about the fates of 'Jews, Social Democrats and Bank-capitalists', but he *was* worried about his future. Like many of his type, his main targets in life were a steady job and a good pension at the end of it all. The Jews and their revolution had been dealt with, but there were still the communists and crackpots like Hitler, with his big trap.* Young as he was, the new recruit knew such types had to be watched.

If Müller was going to survive to enjoy a comfortable retirement on a decent pension he'd have to keep an eye on 'Comrade Laced Boot' from over the border.†

---

* When Drexler, head of the party which would become the National Socialist Party, first heard Hitler speak, he exclaimed in admiration, 'What a trap that man has! We need a chap who can talk like that.'
† The Austrian soldier didn't wear the German jackboot but a laced-up type of mountain boot. Hence the contemptuous name for the Austrians in Bavaria.

TWO

As 1919 gave way to 1920 Müller's concern about the future seemed to be justified. Things were getting worse in Munich, as indeed throughout Germany. There were profiteers and black-marketeers everywhere, battening on the half-starved poor and unemployed. The rich had already smuggled their possessions out into neighbouring Switzerland and were prepared to ride out the storm to come. The mark was becoming progressively worthless. Those who could preferred to accept the dollar or the pound rather than the mark, which was being terminally undermined by the Allies' demand for reparations. When the crunch finally came and Hitler made his first, abortive, bid for power, the humble roll, the mainstay of the poor man's diet of bread and cheap sausage, cost just over three billion marks!

Hitler wrote of those days: 'In Munich it was a sad time. Little light, lots of dirt, unrest, poorly dressed people, impoverished soldiers, in short, the picture resulting from four years of war and the scandal of the revolution.'

Describing the meetings of his comrades in the backroom of the Rosenbad beer house, he asked rhetorically, 'How did we look? Forbidding. Military pants, dyed coats, our feet in remodelled war boots. We were always the same faces. . . . First we received "fraternal greetings" . . . reports were made . . . and then the size of the "treasury" was requested.' Usually it was five marks. Once it reached the dizzy height of seventeen, not enough to buy a single 'half measure' of beer.

47

Later Hitler could laugh at those impoverished times. As yet he had not tapped those sources of wealth which would put him on the road to power. But he was beginning to meet those henchmen – Goering, Hess, Rosenberg, Hoehm, Frank – who would become his 'paladins' and ease him into the salons of the rich and powerful.

The communists were different. They were already receiving large subsidies from Moscow to help them achieve their goal in Germany. For Lenin reasoned that if Germany became communist the whole of Central Europe would. Germany was the Soviets' prime target in those years and the ever-worsening German crisis increased the numbers flocking to the KPD (the German Communist Party). Foolishly, Hans Beimler, the head of the Bavarian KPD, would soon boast, in face of the supposed threat from Hitler's new party, 'If they [the Nazis] want war, then we're ready. We've got the experience of the Eisler Republic behind us,' adding with a knowing sneer, 'We'll meet them again, at Dachau!' Ironically, Beimler himself would. He was one of the first to be sent to Dachau Concentration Camp in 1933.*

Whatever Müller might have thought to the contrary, his political masters, the Social Democrats and his own Bavarian People's Party, which ruled Munich during the '20s, dismissed Hitler and the other right-wing parties as relatively unimportant. The communists, on the other hand, they thought were. They were gaining votes from the socialists rapidly in big cities such as Munich and Augsburg.

Müller, now a member of Bavaria's Political Police, a kind of espionage and counter-terrorist unit which had been common throughout Continental Europe ever since Napoleon's time, was ordered to concentrate his main efforts on the Communists. He was to watch out for Bolshevik infiltrators from Russia, several of whom were Jews; their Communist masters, though some themselves Jews, fondly believed that anyone who spoke Yiddish could pass as a

---

* He escaped to Switzerland, but was killed in action on the Republican side during the Spanish Civil War some time in 1936.

48

German.* Müller was to place his paid informers among their ranks, read their literature and study their organization. Thus the future head of the Gestapo received his early training fighting the Communist underground in Munich. It has been said that Müller went to Moscow to study the methods of the Soviet Secret Police. The author has found no proof of this and it is hardly likely, even during the brief Soviet-German 'honeymoon' of the mid-thirties.

But, at the same time, Müller, while apparently fully occupied with the activities of the Communists, seems also to have kept strict tabs on budding Nazi extremists. Whenever he could, he appears to have made life difficult for them. Nor does he seem to have been exactly gentle with any Nazi suspects he arrested. With them the kid gloves were off. In due course he would not only be feared but hated by members of the Munich Nazi Party. As we will see, they would protest vigorously in the early thirties when he was transferred to the new Gestapo. He himself didn't actually join the Party until 1938, when he was Germany's leading Gestapo agent. Even then he was advised by his boss, Himmler, to accept an SS rank and not one of the high-ranking titles handed out by other branches of the Party.

It was only later that those who have looked into his career began to query his anti-Nazi attitude which continued to the very end of the pre-Nazi period. Indeed, when he was informed that the Nazis were to take over the Munich *Polizeipräsidium*, he drew his revolver and told his old comrades, 'Don't worry, we'll soon see that ratpack off.'

What motivated this strange little man to be so openly anti-Nazi right up to 1933? Was he blind to the realities of the political situation? Did he believe that his cosy little world in Munich, as a member of the Party which ruled the Bavarian capital, with a steady job, married to the daughter of one of the more influential men in the Bavarian People's Party, would go on for ever? How could he afford to treat the Nazis

* Yiddish is based on a 12th-century German dialect, with Hebrew and Polish words added. Slang words in English that come from Yiddish, such as 'nesh' and 'stumm', are really of German origin.

worse than the Communists, who seemingly were everyone's enemy?

Now we can sense that there might have been a good reason for this apparent foolishness. But the world has grown older and more cynical and we see conspiracies in virtually everything that we can't properly understand. Then, back in the early twenties, when, although his political masters seemed to tolerate the extreme right, Müller's attitude might have appeared strange to anyone who thought about it. But in those days when women still wore dirndls and men leather shorts in the streets of the capital, there was only one conspiracy around – that of those international Jewish pluto-crats who had stabbed Germany in the back, and that particular conspiracy theory was strictly the property of Adolf Hitler and his fledgling National Socialist Workers' Party.

By 1923 it was clear to everyone in the know, apart from Hitler's Nazis and other right-wing crackpots, that the pluto-crats who had ruined Germany and were continuing to ruin her were *not* the Jews (though they *were* represented) but Germans and their foreign associates in Western Europe and the United States. For most of these 'conspirators', there was no political advantage to be gained from ruining the defeated country, but there *was* a financial one.

At Versailles it had been determined in 1919 that among the punishments to be inflicted on a defeated Germany was not only the seizure of a fifth of her territory, the reduction of her army to 100,000 men, the abolition of her armaments industry (aircraft, submarine and bacteriological weapons production), but also the imposing of stringent repayments to the victorious Allies for damage to their respective countries during the First World War.

These reparations were crippling, for the worthless mark was not accepted by the Allied powers; they had to be repaid for their suffering with assets that had some value on the inter-national market. But German industry was not in a position to produce the goods that could be exported to purchase the 'hard' currencies the victors demanded. Where would they obtain their raw materials, for example? Who would take worthless marks?

The result was that German industry ceased trying. On the advice, some say, of foreign experts such as Montagu Norman of the Bank of England and the 20th century's most respected economist, the homosexual Maynard Keynes, they and their financial advisers allowed the mark to go into free fall. It was a policy secretly welcomed by Germans with foreign assets and Anglo-Americans with money to buy up German firms for pennies.

The German worker knew nothing of the economic theory. All he knew was that first his savings went, then his disposable goods (mostly to the black market and state pawnbrokers) and finally his wages, if he still had a job. Daily, hourly, the *Reichsmark* lost its value by ten percent, twenty percent, a hundred percent, a thousand, a hundred thousand, a million, a billion.

By October 1923 it took over six million marks to equal one prewar *Reichsmark*. By then the price of a single egg cost the equivalent of thirty million prewar eggs. Women collected their husbands' morning wages at the factory gate in a barrow and hurried off to the shops before the prices went up again so that they could purchase something, anything, for the evening meal.

The government's note-printing plants worked round the clock stamping notes with their new value in a startling bright red. Local governments, even town councils, including that of Munich, issued their own 'emergency money' (*Notstandsgeld*) based, not on gold, but whatever local product still had some tangible value.*

In Baden in Southern Germany that year, heading for a week's skiing holiday that cost him a dollar all in, young Ernest Hemingway talked to a waiter who told him that he had saved up for years to buy a *Gasthaus*. Now all his savings

---

* In his collection the author has such local 'currency', based on the place's pea harvest and even on turnips! At least you could eat those two commodities. Years after, the author, as a young soldier, in common with many others, used caches of such useless money still found in battle-shattered German houses as lavatory paper. It made a change from leaves, grass and 'Army Form Blank'.

would buy were four bottles of champagne. Bitterly, he explained, 'Germany debases her money to cheat the Allies, but what do I get out of it?'

Although economics were never Hitler's strongpoint, he saw that inflation and its catastrophic effects on the man in the street could be of use to him. Conspicuous affluence was rife in Munich. There were 'bloated capitalists' everywhere flaunting their newly gained wealth, living on great estates and in houses in the capital's most fashionable streets, bought for peanuts with foreign currency. The papers were full of stories like that of a half-crazed woman who had left a basketful of money in a shop. Returning to retrieve it, she found the money was still there, but the basket had gone. A factory worker with a salary of two billion marks could afford only to buy potatoes. The multi-billionaire's daily diet consisted of boiled potatoes and white cabbage.

That autumn, with Germany falling apart around him and his party now numbering 35,000 members, with new ones flocking to the crooked cross banner by the hour, Hitler knew the time had to come to act. The year before, his fellow fascist Benito Mussolini had taken a chance. Against all odds he had 'marched' (in fact most of his followers had taken the train) on Rome and, in one bold stroke, seized power. Mussolini had outranked Hitler during the war by one stripe (he'd been a *sargento*), but it showed what a humble working-class ex-NCO could do if he had the guts to take the risk. Well, Hitler, ex-corporal in the Bavarian Royal Army, had the guts. He had his Iron Cross and Wound Medal to prove it. His time had also come to march.

THREE

In the first days of November 1923 Heinrich Müller and his colleagues in the small political police department were placed on semi-alert. In the case of the 'Green Police', the uniformed branch which policed the streets of the capital, all leave was cancelled. There was something in the offing and young detectives like Müller didn't need a crystal ball to guess what it was.

In the city and the surrounding countryside things were getting out of hand. There were strikes everywhere and robberies of food stores were commonplace. Even the farm labourers, normally obedient and God-fearing, were robbing their minimally better-off small-farm bosses and the Army had virtually revolted. They had renounced their oath of loyalty to the central government in Berlin and sworn an illegal one to the Bavarian government until there was a 'change at the top' in Germany. Once again, after nearly five years, there was revolution in the air in Munich.

Hitler, who throughout his career would thrive on crisis, sensed that his time had come. He knew that he had not only his own party behind him but also many other right-wing splinter groups. The latter, however, wanted to play for time. They felt it was necessary to gain the support of the police and the army in Bavaria before they struck. Hitler thought otherwise. Mussolini had gained power without the support of the army or the police; why couldn't he? Besides, he knew that Bavaria's three strong men – Kahr, the State Commissar, the

Bavarian State Police Chief Seisser and Army General Lossow – wanted to bring down the government and also that in Berlin, which ruled the whole of Germany. They thought the time for the Weimar Government to go had arrived, even if it had to be sent packing by force. In essence, the three had the same aims as Hitler, but on a larger scale and with a different timetable.

Hitler, for his part, thought he didn't need these *Monokelfritzen* (Monocle-Fritzes), as he contemptuously named these aristocratic generals who had failed Germany in the First World War and would do the same a quarter of a century later. He decided to go it alone, since he felt that the army and police would not support them in a crisis. If it came to a shooting match, as some of his worried advisers thought it would, the soldiers and the police would not fire on the ordinary working men who made up his Nazi Party, especially as many of his followers had been frontline soldiers, just like the regular police and the soldiers had once been.

Confident that he would win, Hitler picked the evening of 8 November 1923 to start his own march to power. The place was to be the *Bürgerbraukeller*, where on that evening von Kahr himself was scheduled to give a speech to a crowd of 3,000 at which he would denounce Marxism on the fifth anniversary of the November Revolution. As Hitler told his bodyguard Ulrich Graf on the evening of the seventh, 'Bring your pistol. Tomorrow at eight o'clock it's happening.'

8 November dawned cold and windy. In the foothills snow had already begun to fall. Soon there would be heavy snow in the mountains on the Bavarian-Austrian border. Rich Munichers, interested in the new-fangled ski craze, would be soon off on the winding road that led to Berchtesgaden and Obersalzberg and those other Alpine villages which had become fashionable since the English m'lords had invented *Wintersport* for the rich. Hitler had a headache and a bad toothache, but he had no time for a dentist. He told 'Putzi' Hanfstaengl, rich, half-American and Harvard-educated, that there was going to be a revolution which would change everything. Hanfstaengl asked him what would happen to the revolution if he now fell ill. Hitler answered, 'If that should be

the case or if I should die, it will only be a sign that my star has run its course and my mission is fulfilled.'

By the time Hitler's car crossed the River Isar that evening on its way to the meeting in the beerhall his pains had disappeared and he felt ready for anything. He was in a state of barely suppressed tension and Hanfstaengl felt he needed calming down, so he bought three beers for three billion marks.

Now things started to happen. His bodyguard arrived under command of Captain Goering, the wartime flying ace. The twenty police at the door tried to stop the storm troopers, but Goering pulled out his pistol and someone shouted harshly, 'out of the way'. Obediently the police turned and marched out in single file.

Hitler put down his beer, pulled out his own pistol and he and his men surged forward. Now the hall was in an uproar. He fired a shot into the ceiling. There was a shocked silence. The noise of the single shot reverberated round the hall. Then Hitler broke the silence. 'The national revolution has broken out! The hall is surrounded!' No one, he said, was to attempt to leave.

It was the turn of the three strongmen to react. Hitler started towards Seisser's aide who reached into his pocket as if to pull out a pistol. Hitler was quicker. He thrust his own pistol against the man's temple: 'Take your hand out.' With a jerk of his pistol muzzle Hitler indicated that the three strongmen and their two aides should enter a backroom for discussions. Over his shoulder he assured his supporters that everything would be settled within ten minutes.

But he was wrong. The talks went on and on. At one stage Hitler drew out his pistol. Later he said it was part of the game. He told the three generals that it contained four rounds – three for them and one for himself. The gesture was absurd as the prisoners were also being guarded by Hitler's bodyguard Graf, armed with a high-rate machine pistol. He would have mown them down at the slightest provocation, he was that kind of thug.

In the end Hitler, in his shabby frock-coat, looking, as Hanfstaengl thought, like 'a provincial bridegroom', allowed

Kahr to leave on his oath to discuss the matter with the Bavarian government and then return. In his office, the owner of the beerhall was busy totting up his losses. Patriotic he no doubt was, but he was also a practical businessman. Later he was to bill Hitler's Party for 143 steins, 80 glasses, 98 barstools, two music stands and 148 sets of missing cutlery. Obviously, all those present were not as patriotic as German history later tried to represent them.

Naturally Kahr didn't return. The mood in the beerhall was very volatile and Hitler had not appeared to him to be in real control. Besides, he had bigger fish to fry than provincial politics. So he waited, leaving the local Bavarian police to deal with the putschists.

The police hesitated. Frick, Müller's boss at the *Polizeipräsidium*, persuaded his colleagues not to launch an attack, while he hung around the telephone fielding calls from bewildered policemen at the scene of the supposed revolution asking for instructions. Frick had a free hand as Munich's senior burgomaster, Doktor Karl Scharnagl, was a prisoner inside the beerhall, together with most of the other city officials. But already the bigshots were leaving the cellar. Lossow left, so did Seisser. General von Ludendorff, German Commander in the First World War who had gone over to the Nazis and was present in the beerhall, accepted their word that they would return in due course, which of course they didn't. Now it was up to the 'little people' to make the decisions. The generals, the politicians and the high-ranking city officials were keeping their noses out of things. As always in Germany, responsible people in authority seemed to lack what the Germans themselves call *Zivilcourage*.*

By three o'clock the following morning the three key generals had repudiated their undertakings to support Hitler. In an order to be posted publicly, Lossow, for instance, stated he and the others repudiated the Hitler Putsch. Kahr, safely

---

* A difficult word to translate correctly. It means in rough terms what it says: 'civil courage', but it had the connotations of standing up to authority, sticking by one's principles, personal bravery, etc.

protected at the HQ of the 19th Infantry Regiment, prepared a proclamation dissolving the NSDAP and other right-wing organizations, declaring that those responsible for the Putsch would 'ruthlessly be made to suffer the punishment they deserve'. Meanwhile Hitler waited.

Dawn on 9 November was damp, cold and miserable. The snow that fell at intervals reflected the dreary mood of the plotters. Hitler decided his men should be paid. As always in those days of galloping inflation, money had to be fetched daily. SA men were sent to the local note-printing plant of Parcus GmbH. The owners were Jewish, but they allowed them to seize 14,605 trillion marks of inflation currency to pay their comrades. All the same, in true German style, the Parcus Brothers demanded a receipt and got it. It was that kind of revolution.

Time dragged. There were rumours and counter-rumours. Word came in that Captain Roehm, the scarfaced veteran of the SA, had been trapped by the 'Reds' in the city. Then it was discovered the rumour was false. The regular troops were about to mutiny against the government; then they weren't. And so it went on, Hitler seemingly incapable of making a decision. Finally Ludendorff made it for him. They would march from the beerhall to the heart of Munich's government district.

And so they set out on the great adventure. This time there was no brass band. It hadn't been paid, so its members had gone home. Instead, in the lead were the Party bullyboys under Dietrich. They were armed with clubs, rubber hoses, chair legs, ready to tackle the 'Reds' who were supposed to be waiting for them. Dietrich, the ex-sergeant major and butcher by trade, had taken part in one revolution in Munich. Then he had been on the side of the 'Reds', now he fought for the 'Browns', the brown-clad SA. Not that it mattered much, he, like so many of the toughs following Hitler that day, just liked a fight. They were going to get it.

In front of the rank and file came Hitler and Ludendorff in his old-fashioned *pickelhaube* and carrying a dress sword. Like the rabble which he commanded, he was confident that the former soldiers on the other side wouldn't fire on their old supremo. Yet another illusion was going to be shattered this November day.

It began as they started to crowd into the narrow *Residenz-strasse*, breaking ranks and jostling for position. Up front in the *Odeonplatz* they could see armed policemen doubling back and forth. Under the command of Oberleutnant Michael von Godin, the police were trying to erect a makeshift barrier. Now von Godin saw the mob approaching and the barrier wasn't finished. He ordered 'Second Company, double time, march!'

But the sight of the police pushing forward did not stop the SA. One or two of them lunged forward with their bayonets as they had been taught during the war. Von Godin parried a few thrusts with his rifle. All at once a single shot rang out. No one was ever to find out who fired it. Behind von Godin a sergeant reeled and fell dead. 'For a fraction of a second,' he recalled later, 'my company stood frozen. Then, before I could give the order, my people opened fire. It was, in effect, a salvo.'

Immediately that salvo was returned by Dietrich's men and others. Panic erupted. Among the first to fall was Ulrich Graf, Hitler's bodyguard. It is said that Graf dragged Hitler down so hard that his left arm was dislocated. Men started to drag the 'leader' to the pavement. Goering was hit too. Either a bullet or a stone splinter penetrated his crotch, perhaps both. More and more went down on both sides as the wounded were dragged away to be given medical treatment. Now no one was a hero, said Ludendorff. He kept going like a sleep-walker. The police, who had lost four men dead, opened their ranks to allow him through.

So the great putsch had failed. Ludendorff, the hero of the affair so far, now behaved like a spoilt child. He wouldn't allow the police to address him by his rank. 'From now on I am *Herr* Ludendorff,' he insisted, 'as long as these policemen wear a German uniform.' He was led off into oblivion.

Hitler was helped away to be treated. Later he was arrested for high treason. Goering, in great pain, was taken to a house at Number 25 Residenzstrasse. Here the householder, Robert Ballin, was asked if he would give the wounded war hero shelter.

Ballin answered, 'Of course we will give aid and shelter to a wounded man, but I call your attention to the fact that this house is that of Jews.' Goering didn't mind. He was too concerned with the pain he was in. Besides, he was safe here from arrest. Soon he would escape over the mountains to Austria and his years of exile would begin.*

Hitler wasn't so lucky. He was tried and sentenced to imprisonment. Soon he'd be lodged in Cell Number Seven in Landsberg Prison, once occupied by Count Arco-Valley, the half-Jewish right-winger who had started it all when he assassinated Eisner four years earlier.

So it was all over. As the Jewish author Stefan Zweig, who later committed suicide in exile, summed it up, 'In this year, 1923, the swastika and stormtroopers disappeared and the name of Adolf Hitler fell back almost into oblivion. Nobody thought of him any longer as a "possible" in terms of power.' As the world knows to its cost, Zweig was wrong.

* Goering did, however, ensure, when things got bad for the Jews in Germany, that the Ballins were allowed to leave the country safely.

THE MÜLLER FILE
ONE

ONE

In the middle of an October night the little Colonel with twenty-seven years in the US Cavalry behind him stood in the middle of the prison gym and recorded each dead body as it was brought in from the gallows. It was clear to Colonel Burton C. Andrus, commandant of Nuremberg Prison, that the executions had been bungled. Some of the condemned men had been slowly strangled to death by Master Sergeant Woods, the official executioner, instead of having their necks cleanly broken by the fall.

That didn't worry Andrus. Those men who had marched with Hitler in Munich back in 1923 had payed the ultimate penalty and that was as it should be. A few had escaped the gallows, including Hitler himself and Himmler, who had carried 'the Blood Flag' during the March on the Feldherrnhalle. The rest, however, had been properly tried and executed under his supervision. He had taken them over in 1945 at Mondorf in Luxembourg at Camp Ashcan*, as the GIs called it. But there was one more who had cheated the gallows.

Colonel Andrus watched as the squad of GIs under the command of Lieutenant Willis brought the body of the one

---

* The former *Palasthotel* on the banks of the Moselle at Mondorf-les-Bains: one of the two main holding camps for senior Nazis. The place is still there and a careful observer can still see the traces of the iron bars which once covered the windows.

who had escaped the hangman into the gym and laid it down with the rest. Trying to conceal his anger at the German's escape from the noose, he scribbled on his yellow pad, '2.54-carcass delivered'. The printed name against which he wrote those words was 'Goering. H'.

Now he ordered the blanket covering Goering's body to be removed. Official witnesses were brought forward to testify this was really Hitler's one-time right-hand man and that he was truly dead. Thereafter photographs of the bodies were taken by the men of the US Army Signals Corps, both clothed and naked.

Andrus had only hatred for these men, who had marched, failed and then risen to great office, with the power of life or death over 300 million Europeans, in particular for Hermann Goering. That roly-poly tyrant had insulted him personally by committing suicide on the very eve of his execution this 16 October 1946.

But for the time being Goering and the means of his suicide would have to wait. The bodies had to be disposed of. Two trucks rolled into the courtyard outside. They were unmarked and their drivers were never traced afterwards. The Army saw to that. But they were escorted by a heavily armed squad of GIs in steel helmets.

At five that morning, while the citizens of the ruined city of Nuremberg, once the 'City of the Movement' and where the war crime trials had been held,* slept, the trucks set off. They were heading for the *Ostfriedhof* – the East Cemetery – in a suburb of Munich. An American officer had preceded the convoy there, telling the German attendants that trucks would arrive at seven that morning with 'the bodies of eleven American soldiers, killed and buried during the war, whose ashes had been requested by their families'.

In the event the bodies didn't arrive till nine. Their coffins were taken to the crematorium where the fires were already blazing; there were armed US guards everywhere. The

---

* Because the annual rally of the Nazi Party was held there. In the last months of the war the city had been heavily bombed by the RAF and then fought over by the US 7th Army.

German workers were not fooled. By now they'd heard on the radio that Goering had committed suicide and the delay in delivery had been occasioned by an investigation into his suicide. Naturally they hadn't believed the story that they were going to cremate the bodies of fallen GIs. Since when did dead infantrymen warrant an armed guard, officers in attendance and coffins? Dead infantry were simply flung in the nearest available hole, covered with earth and left until the Blacks of the Graves Registration could get to them with their bodybags.

The next day a small group of US officers filed down the steps of US Army Mortuary No.1, the former home of a rich Munich businessman at No 25 Heilmannstrasse. The stairway led from the garden of the villa to the Contwentzbach stream, which flows into the River Isar.

Waiting for them were eleven gleaming aluminium cylinders. They were sixteen inches high and were propped up on the bank. The officers, who had all been sworn to secrecy, went to work. One after another the cylinders were smashed and their contents spilled into the water which would take the ash to the Isar. From there it would go to the Danube and finally to the Black Sea. There would be no memorial left to those who had created the most monstrous regime of the 20th century; even their ashes would vanish.

But there still remained the mystery of Goering's suicide. How had he been able to kill himself on the eve of his execution? He had been supervised twenty-four hours a day, especially after the Head of the Nazi Labour Front, another of the accused, Dr Robert Ley, had choked himself to death the previous October.

On 16 October 1946 Colonel Andrus announced to the newspaper correspondents in Nuremberg: 'Goering was not hanged. He committed suicide at 10.45 last night by taking cyanide of potassium. . . . There were pieces of glass in his mouth and an odour of potassium on his breath.' But where had the poison capsule come from and how had Goering managed to hide it?

Forty-eight hours later, after the forensic team had done their work, Andrus knew the answer to one of those questions.

Their evidence showed that the capsule had been concealed for some of the time in the dead Nazi's rectum. There were traces of faeces on it. Goering had used what the Germans call a *Kassiber* to hide the poison in his anus.

Unable to conceal his anger, Andrus wrote to the Quadripartite Commission on October 28: 'So, in his horrible self-destruction, he was mouthing his own dung.'

But what form had this *Kassiber* taken? Was there any connection between Goering's suicide and that of yet another member of the putsch of 22 years before, Heinrich Himmler? For he, too, had killed himself with cyanide in the form of a capsule before his British captors had been able to stop him. *

Now we know that the glass phial, containing one cc of cyanide, had been concealed in a spent cartridge case, filed to the shape of a small lipstick tube. Then an expansion groove had been cut into it, so that it provided a snug fit and wouldn't fall out of the carrier's anus. Indeed it is recorded that during trials with the device, some of the carriers had found it very difficult to retrieve. In one case the bearer had to be operated on!

More significantly, however, it was discovered that the *Kassiber* poison was not unique. It had not been prepared specifically for Goering. According to German records, now uncovered by Allied intelligence, 950 such devices had been delivered to Gestapo HQ alone in 1944. They had been delivered (and designed) by one of Müller's colleagues, who incidentally had been hunted all over Germany by Müller in the last months of the war until he was finally betrayed by one of his mistresses. Obviously something rather peculiar had been going on at Müller's HQ in Number Ten Prinz Albrecht Strasse in 1944/45.

The man who had ordered the device had been one of the founding members of the Berlin Gestapo, Artur Nebe. Indeed he had been one of the very few National Socialists who had actually served in that dreaded Nazi organization.

---

* The British had spotted the capsule, but before they could stop him Himmler had bitten into it. He died and was buried secretly by a former British council dustbin man, a fitting end.

The ex-lieutenant of engineers was a sharp-tongued professional cop like his future colleague Müller. Indeed some people thought his mind, and his tongue, worked too fast. He was always ready with a smart quip that hurt. Once he remarked, for instance, 'There are no such things as principles, only circumstances'. He had borrowed the phrase from Balzac, but none of his fellow cops were sharp enough to note that, though one of them did remark, 'He will either become a really great man one day or be hanged.' The second option proved to be the correct one.

By the time the Nazis took over, Nebe had thought it better to transfer to the *Kripo* (*Kriminalpolizei*, the equivalent of the detective branch) and as its head he had proved (like Müller) to be the scourge of the communists and other enemies of the state. But in the middle of the war he had joined the mainly military resistance to the Nazis and was particularly involved with Admiral Canaris' *Abwehr* (military intelligence).

It was in these years that Nebe started to have the poison capsules prepared, as well as other items that an agent, or traitor, might need in an emergency, such as false papers. Naturally he had a set prepared for himself. But, though these capsules and papers were manufactured for anti-Nazi plotters, Nebe was nevertheless smart enough to cover himself in case he was found out. The 950 sets of poison capsules and, presumably, sets of false papers were sent to Berlin to prove that Nebe had had them manufactured for legitimate state reasons. It was clear, therefore, that Goering had collected his personal 'L' (for Lethal) pill some time in the spring of 1945 when he had last been in Berlin.*

But although Goering's suicide was soon forgotten, despite the embarrassment it caused the US Army, the fact that there had been some central organization supplying would-be Nazi escapers with poison and papers revived interest in the whole

---

* With his bulk and well-known face, it would have been useless for Goering to ask for false papers. He did, however, collect a second phial of poison, which was found after his suicide in his stored baggage in Nuremberg Jail.

question of what had happened to various missing Nazi war criminals. Even before the war had ended, Anglo-American security/intelligence agents had gone to work in Germany apprehending those on the 'automatic arrest' lists.* in particular these agents were keen to arrest not only the Nazi Party's bigshots such as those tried at Nuremberg but also heads of Germany's Security Organizations.

But as 1945 gave way and Germany was divided into four Zones of Occupation the pursuit of Nazi criminals on the run met with increasing difficulties. The Cold War had already begun. West and East were no longer co-operating behind the scenes. Indeed, both West and East were beginning to recruit war criminals into their own security service. Barbie, the 'Butcher of Lyon', who started to work for the Americans in '46, is the best known example of this new trend – and there were many more minor Nazis thus employed.

All the same, there were approximately 120,000 alleged Nazi war criminals still being sought by the Western authorities. As yet, their names were not known to the general public, but in time they would be. There was Adolf Eichmann of course, and Martin Bormann; and just behind the missing *Reichsleiter* as war criminal number one, the virtually unknown Gestapo Müller.†

After Hugh Trevor-Roper's investigation‡ into the death of Hitler in the Bunker was published in 1946, most authorities had concluded that the Nazi bigshots had died in Berlin that May by their own hand or had been killed by the Russians in one or other of the futile attempts to break out of the trap.

The problem with the Russians and the fact that people

---

* As the author can testify, British Field Security Police, for instance, seemed to have such lists for even the remotest North German village.

† Back in '45 when the Allies had sought Bormann to stand trial at Nuremberg, they had confessed they possessed just one photo of the Führer's 'Brown Eminence'. They were wrong. They had scores of photos of Bormann, but during his Party career he had kept himself so much in the background that nobody had recognized him in these photos.

‡ *The Last Days of Hitler.*

simply wanted to forget the war meant that interest in finding war criminals on the run had waned dramatically after the trials at Nuremberg were over. All the same the issue simply wouldn't go away. Indeed, in some cases, the hunt for the missing war criminals had become a matter of farce. Fourteen days after Goering had avoided the gallows by committing suicide, a German named Joachim Borsburg was found marching somewhat dazed down one of the main streets of nearby Augsburg. He would not have occasioned much surprise – there were a lot of dazed people around – save for one thing. He was dressed in the uniform of a colonel in the *Waffen SS*, something not calculated to make him very popular with the American garrison, especially after the concentration camp revelations at the recent trials.

He was arrested by agents of the US Counter-Intelligence Corps (CIC). But his interrogators found he was no die-hard Nazi or latter-day Rip van Winkle. The explanation was simpler than that. He told the Americans that he had just been promoted to the rank of SS Colonel in a midnight ceremony held, of all places, in the local cemetery.

The CIC agents soon realized that he was mad. A former private in the infantry, he had just been released from a mental home. They asked him as sympathetically as they could who had conducted the promotion ceremony. Confidently Borsburg whispered back, 'Reichsleiter Martin Bormann'.

Borsburg might have been crazy, but where had he learned the name of that high-ranking Nazi who was virtually unknown to the German general public at the time? Borsburg was not alone. There were other reported sightings from people who weren't either mad or sensation-seeking. Heinrich Lienau, a well-known writer in the North German dialect, for example, said he'd spotted Bormann in Luneburg. A Danish doctor reported he'd seen him on the Danish island of Rugen just before the Russians had occupied it. Josef Kleemann, the former socialist head of the German Seaman's Union, claimed he'd sighted him in Sydney, Australia. Even Bormann's brother Albert, Hitler's former adjutant, who had always felt looked down upon by Martin, came out of hiding to state that he wasn't satisfied his brother had died in Berlin as the Allies thought.*

So if Bormann had escaped, we might ask, as did some Allied authorities back in 1946, what about Müller, his supposed friend and helper? No one had seen him die, save one person (of whom we shall soon hear), but he was suspect. He had left the Bunker the day they'd shot SS General Fegelein and had never been seen by the trapped occupants again. Had he gone underground in the ruined city until the heat was off? Had he made a run for it like so many of the Bunker's occupants? A surprising number had managed to escape from within the Soviet ring. Or had he been one of the nameless thousands who had perished in the final battle for the Nazi capital?

---

* He told the author that there had always been 'bad blood' between him and his brother. Over the phone he rapped, 'I'm not talking about him; he had nothing good to say about me when he was alive. I'm not saying anything about him now that he's supposed to be dead.'

70

TWO

Just before he had been betrayed by his aristocratic mistress, the Countess Gisela von Westrop, Dr Kaltenbrunner had one last meeting with SS Colonel Eichmann, now hiding in the Alps. The man who had been in charge of solving the Jewish Problem – once he had remarked, 'I will gladly jump into my grave in the knowledge that five million enemies of the Reich [Jews] have already died like animals' – was not as confident then as he had been when Kaltenbrunner had last seen him in Berlin.

Kaltenbrunner sipped his cognac as he summed his old subordinate up. His face had thinned out and was pale despite the bright May sun outside. He looked worried and sick. 'What are you going to do now?' Kaltenbrunner asked finally.

Eichmann said he'd go into the mountains and make a last stand there with fellow Party faithful.

Kaltenbrunner smiled cynically. 'That's good. Now Himmler can talk to Eisenhower in a different tone. He'll know that Eichmann in the mountains will never surrender, because he can't!'

Irony was wasted on the likes of Eichmann. Still his mouth dropped open. He knew Kaltenbrunner's drunken moods of old, but he'd never heard him so bitter as this.

Abruptly Kaltenbrunner snapped, '*Es ist doch alles Scheisse,*' he growled. 'It's all crap. The game's up.'

Not for Eichmann it wasn't. For his mood was beginning to

change. A week before he had seen his boss Müller in Berlin. A few days before that meeting the latter had offered him fake papers testifying that he had worked for a civilian firm for most of the war. As a young man Eichmann had worked as a salesman for an American oil company and could pass as a civilian in that capacity. 'Well,' Müller had demanded, 'what's up with you? What's it to be?'

By now Müller was a typical cop. He believed in nothing, especially his fellow human beings. He knew they all had their price in the end.

Eichmann faced up to him. '*Gruppenführer*,' he said, 'I don't need the papers.' He tapped his pistol holster. 'This is my certificate. When I see no other way out, it will be my last remedy. I have no need for anything else.'

But Eichmann had been lying to himself then, as he was now in his Alpine refuge. He was not prepared to commit suicide if the worst came to the worst, as he had maintained to Müller. Nor would he fight to death, as he had boasted to Kaltenbrunner. Now he wanted a new identity and the papers that went with it.

Somehow he got them and immediately thereafter he walked boldly into the enemy camp and surrendered. His new papers made him out to be a humble corporal named Barth. It was a typical Gestapo ploy; wanted men employed the '*Flucht nach vorne*'* technique. This was to do the unexpected and catch the enemy off guard. Once inside the sprawling POWs camp of that summer – sometimes holding 50,000 men; POWs were held there in open fields with no facilities – he carried the technique a step further. He confessed to the men screening him that in reality he was an SS officer, *Sturmbannführer* Otto Eckmann.

Eichmann reasoned, correctly, that the enemy would suppose that he was mad or harmless to confess at that time that he was an officer in the SS. Who would guess that Otto Eckmann was really the wanted war criminal Adolf Eichmann? The dodge paid off. After a year in the POW camp,

* Literally 'Flight to the Front'.

he escaped. He worked, apparently, as a farm labourer in the north, far from his Austrian homeland and from Bavaria, to which most of the old-time Nazis had fled. When the coast was clear the SS-run Odessa organization took him up. He was passed down one of that mysterious outfit's 'ratlines' across Germany's southern border into Italy and from thence to South America.

Ricardo Klement, as he was now known, was captured years later by the Israeli Mossad and smuggled back to Israel. To the surprise and astonishment of those who thought Adolf Eichmann long dead, he was put on trial fifteen years later. It had taken a decade and a half to bring the old Third Reich's second most wanted criminal to justice.

But what of his immediate boss, Müller? It seems that, thanks to Nebe, his former colleague and the man he had hunted down, he had been in charge of distributing the *Kripo* Chief's poison capsules and fake papers to the bigshots in Berlin. Müller knew of Eichmann's hideout too. Had he left the Bunker and gone into hiding, either with his mistress or in Eichmann's empty underground den? Then, when the heat had been taken off, had he used Nebe's fake papers, or similar ones, to break out of Berlin to start a new life with a new identity with stolen money and assets he had salted away in Switzerland?* For it was clear that he had been prepared, before the fighting was over, to abandon his Berlin mistress and their children, as well as his long-time wife in Munich and her children. In short, had Müller done a bunk in the summer of 1945 and survived?

By 1946, at the time of Goering's suicide, the Western Allies knew of *Aktion Birkenbaum* (Birch Tree) by which concentration camp inmates who were world-class forgers turned out fake identification papers – birth certificates, marriage licences, passes, etc – for would-be escapers. They knew too that most of the real and forged money (*Aktion*

---

* All the Nazi bigshots, including Hitler, had Swiss bank accounts, even Himmler, the most pedantically correct of the *Prominenz*. While his fellow Nazis stole great estates, Himmler took out a mortgage to pay for his mistress's modest house.

*Bernhard)** had been deposited in the Bavarian/Austrian Tyrol area, sunk into the deep lakes of the area. (As I write this, another 'treasure-seeking operation' is underway there.) So, in essence, those who were still seeking the missing Nazi war criminals knew what to look for and, in general, where.

It is not surprising, therefore, that the only supposed sighting of the vanished Müller was in that area, hundreds of miles from Berlin where he had been last seen. However, that doyen of Nazi hunters, former concentration camp inmate Simon Wiesenthal, who has made it his lifelong task to alert the world to these missing Nazis, only reported this lone sighting several years later. According to Wiesenthal, locals in the Alpine area noted 'a strange lieutenant with the everyday name of Schmidt' in the mountains in late 1945. As Wiesenthal recalled, 'The locals found it strange that a man of about fifty and a humble lieutenant in rank could give orders to high-ranking officers of the SS and Army' still hiding out in the mountains.

In due course the suspicious peasants reported their doubts to the area's American garrison. Under the command of a 'Colonel Pearson', a task force was sent out to apprehend the strange officer. But before the Americans could make contact, they ran into militant Austrian communist partisans. The Americans were forced to fight their way through. (Such things happened on the Austrian borders with Italy and communist Jugoslavia in that year when the communist dictator Tito actually invaded Austria for a short while.) By the time the Americans reached the spot where 'Schmidt-Müller' had been last seen he had vanished. Wiesenthal came to the conclusion that Müller had disappeared with the communist partisans and, in due course, had fled east to his one-time enemies, Russia's communists.

We do not know whether Wiesenthal really believed the peasants' story of Lieutenant Schmidt or whether he was

* This was the forging and, therefore, undermining of the British currency. In the end the Bank of England was forced to withdraw ten percent of its wartime five pound notes due to this clever Nazi ploy, also run from a concentration camp.

using the emerging Cold War scenario to encourage US finance for his own Nazi-hunting operation. If Müller was helping America's new enemy – and later there were genuine cases of former Nazis doing exactly this – then the USA might be prepared to bankroll his one-man campaign against those who had once put him behind the barbed wire of a concentration camp. But there was a catch.

On 17 September 1945 a body was delivered to the former Garrison Cemetery at Berlin-Neukoelln. Here it was buried without ceremony. That autumn bodies were being found by the dozen in Berlin. The remains were placed in Grave Number One, Row Six, of Section Eight of the ex-military burial ground.

How the body got there is not recorded, but the hazy account of the time is that the corpse had originally been interred by one Walter Lueders in the old Jewish Cemetery at Berlin's Grosse Hamburgerstrasse. Who Lueders was is vague, but he is reported to have stated that he had been given the task by the family of the dead man who lived in the area of Berlin's Halleschen Tor. Later, when the corpse was properly identified, it was shown that this could not be true. The dead man's family had never lived in Berlin. Indeed, that year his wife, from whom he had unofficially separated, was earning her keep some three hundred or more miles away in Munich, working in a shop.

At all events, the corpse was finally identified by the CID officer, *Kriminal-obersekretar* Leopold on the basis of his decorations, his papers and a few other items. These items were sent to the dead man's widow in Munich. But they didn't help her or the authorities much with further identification. For by the time they did reach the shop assistant, supporting her two children the best she could in that terrible time of black market and starvation, the documents lacked any photographs of her supposed husband.

All the same the Berlin Central Registry went ahead and registered the death on 15 December 1945 under the number 11706/45. Who occasioned that registration without any further proof of the dead man's identification, save that of a former Nazi policeman, is not known today.

75

And there the grave remains to this day, though it has been disturbed three times since that December over half a century ago. Twice when the mouldering remains were dug up for examination and once to have a headstone in black marble placed on top of it.

Undecorated by the gold cross, usual on the gravestones of German catholics, the inscription reads:

UNSER LIEBER VATI
HEINRICH MÜLLER
GEB.28.4.1900.
GEF.BERLIN MAI 1945*

It seems, therefore, that Wiesenthal's solution had not been too accurate. For that December 1945 registration of the supposed Müller body in Berlin brought ever more problems with it than just the mystery of how he had reached the Austrian Alps disguised as *Leutnant* Schmidt.

Where had the corpse been for those three months after the flight from the Bunker and its interment in that old Jewish Cemetery (a macabre joke in itself)? And who was Walter Lueders who, single-handed, buried the body there? There is a possible explanation for the corpse's transfer from the Jewish burial ground to that of the Berlin Garrison. But why had someone like an already suspect *Kriminalobersekretar* Leopold, who presumably would have wanted to keep his head down in 1945, stepped forward to give a positive explanation? And why had Müller's photos been removed from the identification papers sent to his widow in Munich? Above all, who had paid for that gravestone and had come, year in, year out, for a decade or more to place flowers on the slab with that significant dedication – 'KILLED IN ACTION, MAY 1945'? 'May' – the only definite statement, save for the date of birth, in the whole business.

* For our dear Father, Heinrich Müller. Born 28.4.1900. Killed in action, Berlin, May 1945.

1934: THE NIGHT OF THE LONG KNIVES.

'Hate is a much more powerful emotion than love'

SS Gruppenführer Heydrich to his wife, Lina

ONE

It was the Professor's misfortune that he lived in a German state at a time when anti-semitism was already well established. Despite the fact that his wife was a staunch Catholic and he himself a great admirer of Wagner, he was still regarded as a Jew.

Bruno, which was his first name, didn't look particularly Jewish. He didn't help matters, however, in his occasional musical performances, by frequently slipping into the role of what his fellow citizens called an 'Isidor': a caricature of a Jew. As one of his acquaintances recalled long afterwards, 'Most of the inhabitants of Halle had not the slightest doubt about his Jewish origin.'

Nor did it help much that, after the death of Bruno's natural father, his mother had married a prosperous locksmith with the unfortunate name of Suess; everyone knew *that* was a Jewish name.*

We do not know how Bruno Suess-Heydrich felt about his alleged Jewishness. Outwardly he seemed to make a joke of it. What is important for us is the impact that his supposed Jewish antecedents had on Bruno's second son born in Halle on 7 March 1904. The boy was christened Reinhard Tristan after the character in Wagner's opera *Tristan and Isolde*. With his blond hair and cold blue eyes, he certainly fitted the

---

* *Jud-Suess*, based on a novel about a real-life medieval character, was made into an anti-semitic movie during the Second World War.

stereotype of the Nordic hero, as advocated by the leaders of the Nazi Party in years to come.*

'Reini', as his family nicknamed him, was intended for a musical career like his father. But that wasn't to be. Although he learned to play the violin well, he was an awkward child when outside the family circle. He had a quick temper and was inclined to strike out swiftly when teased. And he was teased often. He had a high-pitched voice which earned him the nickname of 'Ziege' (billy-goat) at school and he was often taunted on account of his supposed Jewishness. Here and at the Gymnasium, he earned the soubriquet which followed him most of his early life – 'Izzy'.

Young Heydrich soon learned that he wasn't going to make much impression on the world unless he did something positive about it. He was awkward, was cursed with a falsetto voice and fat feminine hips. Nor was he particularly interested in sport, though in his early manhood he did fence for Germany at championship level and secretly learn to fly. He knew that if he was not going to be treated like a worm for the rest of his life he would have to make people fear him, even hate him if necessary. He'd have to be tougher, crueller, more ambitious than the rest.

As a high-school boy he took to walking to and from school with one foot on the pavement and one in the gutter. He never deflected from this straight course, even for an adult. Generally people got out of his way when they saw him coming. If they didn't and objected, he'd pitch into them, however big and tough.

He also started to show off. Once he climbed on the roof of the Gymnasium, three floors above the schoolyard, and, in full view of the horrified staff, walked slowly along the gutter in a mock balancing act.†

* As has often been pointed out, hardly any of the Party bigshots fitted the type.
† In 1934 he repeated the show when, as Germany's representative to Interpol, he discovered that the Swiss hotel in which the delegates were staying was not flying the new swastika banner. In complete darkness that night he shinned up the façade of the building carrying the German flag to shock the Swiss the next morning when they discovered it.

When he joined the German Navy as an officer cadet in March 1922 he found an outlet for his aggressiveness, especially in fencing which he now took up. All the same on his first leave in Halle he was greeted by the mocking cries of his former schoolmates: 'Look, there's Izzy Suess in naval uniform!' But Heydrich told his brother, 'There's nothing I can do about it.' Even his classmates of 'Crew 22', as his year was called, rejected him. His sense of isolation and rejection must have grown ever deeper. One day, however, he'd pay them all back. It wouldn't do to cross Izzy Suess.

So he grew older and bolder. He wasn't liked, but he was an excellent officer, technically gifted and was commissioned into the signals branch of the tiny German Navy, restricted in numbers, ships and weapons by the strictures of the *Versaillesdiktat*, as right-wing Germans called the Versailles Peace Treaty bitterly. He also attempted to prove his masculinity by his many affairs, mostly with harbour whores who hung around sailors. Often he would boast when he was drunk, 'I've had 'em all, black, brown, white, even yellow.'

But in the end his womanizing became his downfall. In 1931 he was called before a court of honour because he had broken the naval code of honour (*Ehrenkodex*). He had slept with a young woman of good family, whom he had promised to marry but had then jilted. The Court had found against him and that year, at the height of the German Depression, with six million Germans out of a population of some eighty million unemployed, Heydrich was cashiered.

What was he to do? How could a naval officer, trained in signals and how to kill at sea, find a new job in times like these? He had not reckoned on Lina von Osten, now his fiancée, who, despite her aristocratic title, was the daughter of a poor primary school teacher on the North German island of Fehmarn. She was a tough young woman and right-wing to boot.

While Heydrich bewailed his fate (His brother Heinz had given up studies and was trying to earn his living as a casual labourer, while his 70-year-old father was struggling in Halle to keep his head above water) Lina acted. She contacted an uncle who had influence in the Nazi Party. In particular, he

81

was well-known to a weak-chinned ex-chicken-farmer who had carried the 'Blood Banner' at the abortive Munich Putsch of 1923. Now, nearly a decade later, Heinrich Himmler had the grandiose-sounding title of *Reichsführer SS*, but it didn't mean very much; his SS were overshadowed by Captain Roehm's bully boys, the Storm Troopers, who were nearly half a million strong. Still the pedantic Bavarian was ambitious and had great plans for his SS. With money now flowing into the Party's coffers from the great German industrialists, who felt the Nazis presented the last bulwark against the communists and other socialist crackpots, Himmler was recruiting. Lina hoped that Reinhard might be one of those new recruits, who were actually paid a salary, however small.

At first Himmler didn't want to see Heydrich, but in the end he agreed to a twenty-minute interview. He seemingly liked the appearance of the Aryan-looking applicant and was pleased to hear that Heydrich was a former officer. When, however, he heard that Heydrich had served as a *Nachrichtenoffizier* Himmler's sallow face lit up and he decided to put the would-be new recruit to the test.

'*Nachrichten*' can mean both 'signals' and 'intelligence'*. Himmler now took it that Heydrich had been a naval intelligence officer and he had already planned to institute an SS intelligence unit, a kind of secret service, which was lacking at that time in the Party. He explained his plan for such an organization to Heydrich, ending with, 'If you think you can do it [draw up a plan for an SS Intelligence Service], go away for twenty minutes and sketch out your scheme. Show me how you would go about it.'

Heydrich was quick on the uptake. He didn't correct Himmler. Instead he went into another room and racked his brain for a few moments before getting down to the problem. At that time he would have done anything to obtain a paying job. He had received a few hours' training in naval intelligence and he had long been an avid reader of English spy novels. Using this background and a lot of important-looking naval terminology, he presented his plan to Himmler and in

* Basically the word means 'news'.

a few days was accepted. He was posted as an ordinary SS man to the Hamburg branch of the 'Black Guards' and, as Himmler described that time in Heydrich's funeral eulogy in 1942, 'He stayed in Hamburg, side by side with out-of-work lads, taking part in the beer cellar brawls in the red-light districts of that city. Then I called him to Munich and gave him a job in the as yet small leadership group at the Party HQ.'

Small it was and the pay was not very generous either. For a while the now-married Reinhard and Lina shared their flat with the SS office and staff. The highpoint of their day was 'when we had the staff lunch. It was usually *weisswurst*, mustard, a roll, washed down with half a litre of beer. But it kept back the pangs of hunger.'[*]

Heydrich took to his new job like a fish to water. Now 29 years old, he was not particularly interested in the Nazi Party; he was interested in rooting out secrets – those of Party members or of the opposition – which would give him the power over people that he craved. One day soon anyone daring to call him 'Izzy' was going to regret it, if he lived that long.

Now, in 1933, Heydrich made his first major step towards power. In January of that year Hitler had become German Reich Chancellor. Two months later he and his Party also controlled the State of Bavaria and Himmler, who, with his SS, had gradually taken over police power in other parts of Germany from Hamburg to Hesse, became Police Commander of the whole of Bavaria on 1 April. With him, Heydrich, head of Secret Service and Police (*SD*), now took over what would become, at first, the Bavarian Political Police. Now, for the first time, as far as is known, Heydrich came into contact with Chief Inspector Heinrich Müller, one day to be known throughout Occupied Europe as 'Gestapo' Müller.

The latter, a cop now for fourteen years, must have been a very worried man that spring when the 'New Order' arrived in Munich. Although he had mainly been concerned with, or

---

[*] Lina Heydrich to the author. '*Weisswurst* (white sausage) is and was a speciality of the area and Frau Heydrich wasn't particularly keen on it, 'but it was better than hunger any day'.

rather hunting down, key communists, the Nazis' greatest political opponents, he was detested by the local Party and, in particular, the Nazi Storm Troopers.

As the Upper Bavarian and Munich Party HQ reported on Müller that year: 'He is a most violent opponent of communism, who at times disregards legal rules and regulations. . . . It is, however, equally clear that, had it been his job, Müller would have similarly acted against the right wing. Being incredibly ambitious, he would be bent on recognition from his superiors under any system.'

It was an opinion shared by Rudolf Hess, who had helped the Führer write his *Mein Kampf* and was soon to be appointed the Führer's Deputy. He saw Müller as a ruthless careerist who would let no one stand in his way and took the 'credit for other people's work'.

In essence, Munich Nazi Party HQ doubted if a policeman like Müller had any professional future in the New Germany, especially in a sensitive secret police spot. He was a traditional police 'plodder', an assiduous Catholic churchgoer, who contributed his routine forty pfennigs to the Party's *Eintopfspende.** Worse, he was the son-in-law of the Bavarian People's Party bigshot, Dischner, who published his own Party newspaper. As the head of the Nazi Party in the suburb of Munich-Pasing, where Müller had been born and now lived for a while, concluded, 'we can hardly imagine him as a member of the Party'.

Müller's reactions at the possibility of being thrown out of the only career he had known since his military service nearly two decades before are not recorded. But we can guess that the man who had boasted to his colleague Franz Josef Huber, 'if they [the Nazis] try to take over, we'll soon see them off,' must have been deeply shocked when Huber received his 'blue letter' that month. The 'blue letter'† indicated that he

---

* Supposedly a fund to raise money for the new 'one-dish lunch' for the poor and Party brass alike. In reality, it was used to collect funds for the Nazis.
† Envelope and letter of that colour, used in schools to indicate a child had not been promoted to the next class; in this case it meant dismissal.

had been fired, though Heydrich re-instated him. Now, with hundreds of old-time policemen being released all over Germany because they had voted the wrong Party ticket, Müller guessed he'd be next. He was in for a surprise.

As Himmler once remarked of his subordinate, 'Heydrich possessed an infallible nose for men. He saw the ways which friend and foe would take with a clarity that was amazing. His colleagues hardly dare lie to him.'

Now Heydrich tackled the problem of these old-time professional cops. To a great extent he had been disappointed by the young men he had personally recruited into the secret police organization that would soon become the Gestapo. They were all 'uniforms and parades' and, as Heydrich expressed himself angrily in 1933, 'The time for marching is over. Let's get down to work.'

These older men, who had undergone good solid training, were different. Besides they had had the experience, those long dreary hours of watching, waiting and assessing that make a good detective. As he told his wife, he was sick of the 'stupid Storm Troopers. We've got to ensure that the SS doesn't become another SA [Storm Troop Organization].' Heydrich wanted to give the SS a real task for the future and he felt it should be the protection of the new state. How? Through *his* secret police.

As the Israeli Attorney-General Gideon Hausner said of Heydrich at the opening of Eichmann's Trial in Jerusalem in 1961, 'Heydrich always contended, "One must know as much as possible about people". He was happy to receive any information whatsoever about economic developments, social life, politics and *especially about the private lives of Party members*. Heydrich wanted to know every possible detail about the members of the Party and their opponents, everything relating to their character and their weaknesses, every item that might be possibly used against a man or institution, *especially if it might be used as a threat for purposes of blackmail*.

'Nothing in the more intimate lives of all the leaders of the Reich and afterwards of the leaders and administrators of the whole of Europe escaped the vigilance of the SD. Clearly, such an instrument soon became a weapon of great strength.'

What better men could he find for this task than the old-school detectives of Müller's kind; they would know the deepest secrets, even those of Hitler himself, of 'old fighters'* who had reformed and led the Party from Munich for the last decade. Naturally Heydrich knew he would face fierce opposition from these same Party hacks whom he despised privately. Even the new Gauleiter of Munich, Wagner, opposed the appointment. As late as 1937 the Munich Party HQ was writing to Himmler about the hated Müller. The complaint stated that he had always 'tried to curry favour with his superiors by a particularly vigilant persecution of National Socialists.' He had even referred to the 'Great Leader' as an 'immigrant unemployed housepainter' and an 'Austrian draft dodger'.

None of these things impressed or influenced Heydrich, who was determined to have Müller and his anti-Nazi cronies in his new organization, which he hoped one day would document the life of every German man, woman and child *von der Wiege bis zur Bahre'* (from the cradle to the grave). That spring he allowed the Bavarian newspapers to publish the fact that over 300 communists and anti-Nazis had been arrested in Munich area and were being sent to the first 're-education camp', also known as a concentration camp, after the concept first instituted by the English during the Boer War.† Heydrich was referring to Dachau.

So Müller was appointed. On the surface he was Heydrich's creature. After all he had good reason to be grateful to the younger man, who had just saved his bacon – on the surface! But whereas Heydrich at times gave way to his overweening vanity and boasted about his feelings and plans, Müller kept his thoughts to himself. He had long learned that the average

---

* *Alter Kämpfer*, the old warrior, ie a Party member who had fought for Hitler before he had been elected Reich Chancellor in '33.
† Lord Kitchener's internment camps for the women and children of rebel Boers. It is often said that Heydrich was the organizer of the first concentration camp, but that doubtful honour seemed to have gone to Dr Frank, the future Nazi governor of Poland, executed at Nuremberg.

German talked too much as it was, something he had often found useful in his career as a detective. Occasionally among his cronies, Huber, Meisinger and the like, of the now defunct Bavarian Political Police, he had unburdened himself, but not now.

For not only had he Heydrich as a new boss but he was being transferred to Berlin, the home of the 'Sow Prussians', whom no good Bavarian would trust. Now he was to start off on his meteoric career which would make him an SS general within six years and gain for him a title that would ensure that he was remembered long after he disappeared on that April day in 1945 when all appeared to have been lost.

Yet, for all that was ever discovered about him when he ruled the world's most feared police organization, the Gestapo, Müller is as remote as he was when Heydrich first interviewed him.

TWO

Putzi Hanfstaengl, Hitler's backer and PR man during most of the 20s, had been about to leave Munich for the 25th reunion of his Harvard Class in the USA when he had occasion to drop in at the Munich HQ of the SA, commanded by Hauptmann Ernst Roehm, whom he had known since the early days of the Party. Roehm was a veteran soldier with a scar on his cheek and the end of his nose shot off, legacies of the First World War. The son of a railway clerk, he had nonetheless achieved the rank of captain in the old Bavarian Royal Army, no mean feat in those class-conscious days. But then, as he wrote himself, 'I had only one thought and wish from my childhood – to be a soldier.' Now, retired from the old Bavarian Army, he had formed a new one, the Storm Troopers (the SA) which had been the militant mainstay of Hitler's bid for power.*

Hanfstaengl was made to wait in the foyer of the HQ. There seemed to be some sort of party going on, he could hear the clink of glasses, the sound of music and loud voices. Obediently he waited. Roehm was a powerful man these days; it didn't do to cross him. Some within the Party whispered behind his back that he was getting too big for his highly polished boots.

As he waited, 'My eyes roamed over the opulent furnishings and carpets. Believe it or not there were even Gobelin

---

* Before it was brought to heel, the SA numbered about 4 million members.

88

tapestries on the walls. You know, it looked like a millionaire's brothel.' *

Suddenly Hanfstaengl was shocked out of his reverie by the door flying open to reveal 'Roehm, tunic unbuttoned and his round face shining with sweat. He was breathing heavily and tottered unsteadily, obviously drunk. His arm was draped round the shoulders of a young boy – *completely naked*. My God, I thought the rumours are true.'

In latter years Putzi made a living peddling sexual rumours about the perverted love life of the Nazi bigshots. He was, with Otto Strasser, another founder member of the Nazi Party, one of the main sources for a report on Hitler's perverted make-up commissioned secretly by the OSS, forerunner of the CIA, in 1943. But in this case Putzi was right. Roehm was a notorious homosexual and didn't give a damn who knew it. He even kept a tame Munich lawyer occupied full-time dealing with the many threatening letters and blackmail attempts that regularly came to his office as a result. (Homosexuality was illegal under Paragraph 175 of the German Legal Code.)

But one man in Munich who was in the know about Roehm's homosexual love life couldn't be brow-beaten by legal threats. He was, indeed, the law himself when the last pre-Nazi take-over scandal broke in 1932. It concerned Roehm's paid pimp and homosexual, Peter Granninger. Granninger, unemployed and prepared to do anything to earn a dishonest living, had allowed Roehm to practise fellatio on him in 1928. Thereafter (the pimp was now a member of an 'SA Intelligence unit') he ran seven apartments in the Munich area where Roehm met the boys who Granninger procured for him. Most of them were from the Gisella High School and Granninger had taken to waiting at the school gate for likely pretty boys whom he paid for fellatio before passing on the 'best performers' to Roehm.

The man who knew was Müller. Of course he realized that Hitler must have long known about Roehm's activities. Bavaria had always been used to hiding sexual scandals. It is,

* To the author.

after all, a Catholic state, and as is usually the case where the prelates hold power, the sexual aberrations of bigshots are quietly swept beneath the carpet. In Bavaria it seems still to be true.

But in 1933 Hitler was not just another politician; he was master of the Reich. Roehm, for his part, was the head of a huge and troublesome para-military organization which was challenging the ultra-conservative but very small German Army, the 100,000-man strong *Reichswehr*. Besides, Himmler, with his grandiose title of *Reichsführer SS* which meant nothing, was envious of Roehm and the power he wielded through his Storm Troopers and wanted to be rid of him. But although he knew that he'd have the support of the *Reichswehr* and, ultimately, the Führer himself, he knew too that he'd have to blacken Roehm's personal character in the eyes of the German people. Homosexuality, especially with young boys, was the ideal way to do so.

Thus the 'new boy', hated as he was by the SA, started to prove his worth right from the start.

Meanwhile, at a much higher level, the Party bigshots, who like Mafia bosses were always jostling around the *Capo** for new positions and places of more influence, were coming together in a secret campaign to rid the beloved Leader from the 'perverted stigma' of Roehm.

At first Himmler had been hesitant. As we have seen, despite his title, he was only a little fish, whose private army, the SS, amounted only to a fragment of the size of Roehm's SA. But when, gradually, Goering, the most powerful man after Hitler, came out as an opponent of Roehm's plans for the 'New Germany', he joined the plotters wholeheartedly. Hess was next. He took a moral stance, apparently detesting Roehm's well-known homosexuality, despite the fact that he was suspected of homosexuality himself and was called *'Tunte'* (a corruption of the German word for aunt, meaning homosexual) behind his back. Even Hitler himself was worried about the effect of Roehm's outspoken comments on

* Interestingly enough, the Mafia word was used in the concentration camps (*Kapo* in German) for the convict bosses behind the barbed wire.

big business and the Army, for he would need both in due course. The stage was being set for a final reckoning with *Hauptmann* Ernst Roehm and his private army, the Storm Troopers of the SA.

By April 1934, in his new office at 103 Wilhelmstrasse, Berlin, Heydrich had virtually taken over the new Gestapo and was, under Himmler, responsible for the whole of the secret police throughout the various German states. At the age of thirty he had become one of the key, if little-known, figures in the Third Reich. He knew that, as a 'Party upstart', he had powerful enemies, but he knew too that his star was in the ascendacy. Müller felt the same. He was prepared to do his utmost to enable his 'Prussian' chief to achieve his aims, for it would be to his advantage to do so.

Two months later, on 6 June 1934, ten years before the D-Day invasion which began the downfall of the Nazi empire, Hitler ordered that every Party official, including all heads of Party organizations, must furnish the SD with all the information it required. For Heydrich and his detectives this was a tremendous step forward. It meant they were officially empowered by the Führer himself to enquire into the affairs of the SA, political and personal, to furnish the evidence which would be needed to break the power of Roehm and his brown-shirted thugs who, with nothing else to do now that the Party had achieved power, were making a public nuisance of themselves on the streets of Berlin virtually every day.

By the third week of June Heydrich, Müller and the rest of the senior men in the Gestapo and the SD were compiling lists of SA men and other 'enemies of the state'. (One was General von Kahr who had betrayed the Führer so long ago in the Munich beer cellar.) They would be 'eliminated' as soon as the Führer gave the order. Secretly, Heydrich gave Müller and his cronies of the Bavarian Political Police another order. They were to watch the SD officers entrusted with drawing up what would be the 'death lists' in case they betrayed them to Himmler's enemies. As always, Heydrich trusted no one. Neither did Müller, but it must have pleased him no end that, not only was he playing a small part in the liquidation of his old Munich enemies, the SA, but also he might have a role in doing the same thing with the 'new boys' of the SD in their flashy black uniforms and their aristocratic Austrian titles. The *'Herr Doktors'* and *'Herr Barons'* – all Austrians seemed to have titles of one sort or another – might be in for a surprise yet.

In the end, however, it was Roehm who surprised Heydrich and Müller. On 1 May 1934 the *Reichswehr*, and naturally the Führer, had pulled off a coup which was analyzed as a deliberate slight to Roehm's SA. At the great May Day Parade in Berlin the *Reichswehr* contingent had marched wearing the new swastika and eagle badge of the future *Wehrmacht*. But it was not simply a change in uniform, beloved by all those who run armies, it was a provocation. Those who could interpret such matters realized that Hitler was sending a covert message to Roehm. The *Reichswehr* was the Party's armed force, not the SA. Roehm was never going to take over the Army, as he seemingly planned to do.

But Roehm, who was one of the few Party bigshots who addressed the Leader with the 'thou' form (*duzen*), was no tame subordinate who simply accepted the Führer's *diktat*. Some time in early June his spokesman announced that, with effect from 1 July, the whole of the SA would go on annual leave. Roehm, for his part, would leave Berlin for a health farm (*Kur*) at the little resort town of Bad Wiesee, south of Munich. That announcement was probably made to indicate to Hitler that the SA leadership wanted time to think over their position in this New Order.

Be that as it may, Heydrich seized upon the announcement eagerly. For him the announcement could mean only one thing: the SA was dispersing from public sight while the organization's leadership planned a *coup d'etat*. After all, the SA outnumbered the regular army by at least three to one and many of its members were *Frontsoldaten* who had combat experience and knew how to use the weapons they kept in their own private arsenals. Behind the scenes Heydrich began to pull strings. Rumours of treachery and armed revolt spread through army officers' messes and Party headquarters, right up to the Reich President Field Marshal von Hindenburg himself.

Hitler heard them and grew nervous. He really began to believe that his old comrade was up to something. Roehm, flamboyant homosexual that he was, had always been a very brave soldier. He had risked death in the trenches and had never been scared of mixing it in the beerhall brawls of the early days. Rapidly Hitler began to fall into Heydrich's hands. Every sign was that the Führer was ready to take decisive action against Roehm and the SA.

That June those who knew Hitler from the old days could see that his nerves were going. 'I saw at a glance, the moment he arrived, that he wasn't the sort of guest you needed at a wedding,' *Gauleiter* Florian said, remembering Hitler's presence at the marriage of his fellow *Gauleiter* Terboven.* 'His face was twitching, morose. He was a bundle of nerves. Couldn't listen to a conversation. Walked off in the middle of the ceremony.'

According to Florian, in his old age still a great admirer of the man who had led Germany to its doom, 'See that chair over there. That was the chair in which the Führer always sat when he came to visit me at my Düsseldorf HQ.' Terboven and Hitler then began a heated conversation about something unknown to him, but he guessed that his fellow *Gauleiter* was asking Hitler to do something very drastic. He was. Some time before, Terboven, who knew of the alleged SA plot, had pleaded with Hitler: 'Go down there [Bavaria] and clear the lot of them out.'†

Hitler appeared to refuse until finally 'Pili' Koerner of Goering's staff appeared and announced that he had just flown from Berlin at the Party boss's command. For Himmler had informed Goering, 'The SA is arming for revolt!'

That did it. Hitler's reaction was explosive.

As Florian recorded, he exclaimed, '"That's it! I've had enough." His face was suffused with rage and I thought he

---

* In conversation with the author.
† According to Frau Schwaebe, wife of the publisher of the Nazi *Westdeutscher Beobachter.* She told the author she had spoken to Terboven about the wedding incident in 1943 when they had been together at the winter sports spa of Winterberg.

might have a stroke at any moment. But he didn't. Instead he shouted: "I'll make an example of them all."'

Now things happened fast. On 30 June the Gestapo and SD started making arrests of key SA leaders all over the Reich. Müller and his friends had done their job well. They were prepared. In Munich, 'Sepp' Dietrich, the head of the *Leinstandarte*, one day to be an Army Group Commander, used two companies of his Bodyguard Regiment to carry out his special job. He wasn't just going to arrest the SA 'mutineers', he was going to shoot them.

As far as this author can ascertain, Hitler never signed a written order to have his old comrades and a few of his enemies killed between 30 June and 2 July 1934 – 'the Night of the Long Knives', as it had gone down in history. But just as with the origin of the Holocaust, which preoccupies historians of the period to this day, perhaps Hitler's expression carried as much weight as his signature.

Herr Schwaebe, editor of the *Westdeutscher Beobachter*, remembers seeing Hitler briefly at the start of the forty-eight hours of official murder in which some 200 Germans were liquidated without trial. They met in Cologne where Schwaebe published his newspaper. Hitler, 'pale-faced and haggard', shook hands, but didn't say a word. Instead he hurried to the waiting car. Schwaebe, according to his own words,* watched him, then he got into his own car and set off for his publishing office,' with the sky over the twin spires of the Cathedral and the sleeping rooftops a blood red. . . . I knew there'd be need for a special edition in the morning.'

* To the author.

94

THREE

By the afternoon of Monday, 2 July it was all over. Roehm had been 'dealt with' at Munich Stadelheim Prison and the alleged revolution had been averted.

Hitler was pleased with the outcome. A year later he confessed to his military adjutant that he still 'treasured' the document on the would-be traitors which had been provided by Heydrich. From then onwards it was whispered behind the Führer's back that Heydrich could be relied upon to provide any evidence the Führer wanted – true *or false*!

Heydrich's star was now in the ascendant, and with it that of Müller. Heydrich's role in the 'Night of the Long Knives' was rewarded, with Himmler making him a *SS Gruppenführer*, roughly a lieutenant-general, not bad for a humble naval lieutenant who had been cashiered half a decade before.

Müller's contributions to those SA dossiers were honoured too. Now, with the SS independent of the discredited SA, Heydrich started reorganizing his police. Himmler gave him his head. For that ineffectual bureaucrat could now indulge himself in his racial nonsense: the origin of the Indo-Germanic languages, the source of the supposed Aryan race, the role of Henry the Fowler and all the rest of the New Order rubbish. (When Sergeant Adolf Eichmann of the SS requested permission to marry, for instance, not only had he to have his racial purity attested, but his poor wife-to-be had to prove her ability to bear Aryan children by means of an embarrassing and protracted vaginal examination. To those in the know and of a cynical disposition, such as Müller, it must have all seemed a dreadful waste of time, especially as the future *Frau Scharführer Eichmann* was already pregnant.) Müller was made one of the two section heads in Sub-Department (II) which came directly under the control of Heydrich, who preferred to retain control of Gestapo Department (II).

Müller was given carte blanche by Heydrich. For the next two years his main target would be the communists. After all, he was regarded by Himmler and Heydrich as their 'communist expert'.

In the last general election the communist party (the KPD) had registered almost as many votes as the Nazis themselves. The socialists (the SPD) had really outdone both of them, but Nazi cunning and skilled wheeling-and-dealing had ensured that Hitler's party would be the main force in the *Reichstag*. Now the KPD was banned. But it was better prepared for underground anti-Nazi activity than the socialists who went over to the Nazis in droves. Besides, the KPD was funded and, to some extent, directed by the Russian communists, who knew a great deal from their own activities in the pre-revolutionary period about illegal activities.

For a while Heydrich had considered sending some of the professionals from Munich to the new concentration camp in Dachau, but the fact that they had worked so hard for him in the 'Roehm Affair' had changed that. Besides, he now valued the professionals and they began working for him, the former enemy, with a will.

That must have pleased Heydrich. For it proved a theory of his: anyone would work for him, whatever his political outlook, if the reward, or threat, was right. As one of his academic recruits, Werner Best, recorded after the war, 'We were all astonished by the way that all of Heydrich's subordinates feared the Chief, but at the same time had a certain respect for him.'

They were also prepared to do all kinds of dirty work for their chief. One year after the Roehm Affair, Heydrich recruited another young academic to his staff. He was *Herr*

Doktor Walter Schellenberg, a smart Saarlander, who had been a duellist and leader of Nazi student organizations at university. Schellenberg, who would rise to become an SS general and head of the combined SS-Army Intelligence Service, was also very handsome in a cocky, smooth-talking way.

At that time Heydrich had installed his wife and two young children in a new house on her native island of Fehmarn, while he remained in Berlin. At weekends he flew to the nearest airfield to visit her, returning on Sunday to his weekday debauchery, including sessions with the whores he had installed in the SS's own spy brothel 'Salon Kitty', used for pumping secrets out of prominent Germans and foreigners who also frequented the place.

Thus it came about that one weekend Heydrich used his Fehmarn base (it's still there in the form of a beach house, where till her death Frau Heydrich used to sell beer, goulash and sausages to day-trippers) for a conference of his subordinates, including the new boy Schellenberg. After the conference Heydrich changed his plans and flew straight back to Berlin, leaving Schellenberg to kick his heels on the island with only Frau Heydrich for company. Still Heydrich was the boss and he did as he was told.

When he finally returned to Berlin, he was approached by his official superior, Müller, now called 'Stapo Müller'. The latter told the new boy that he and the Chief were going out on a spree that night 'in mufti'. Schellenberg had been granted the honour of accompanying them.

That night the three of them had supper in Berlin's Alexanderplatz. Naturally there was plenty to drink. Heydrich and Müller were both proud of their ability to tip 'more than one behind the collar stud'. Thereafter they went to a bar and had more to drink. Suddenly Müller asked, as he had been prompted to by Heydrich: 'Well, how did you get on at Ploen Lake?' He meant the great inland lake in Schleswig-Holstein 'Did you have a good time?'

Heydrich listened but said nothing. Schellenberg, who was always quick on the uptake, noticed, however, that the Chief had gone very pale. Still he didn't tumble to what Müller was hinting at and asked if Müller was asking about his afternoon excursion to the lake with Frau Heydrich.

Now Heydrich broke in. 'In a cold sibilant voice he said, "You have drunk some poison. It could kill you within six hours. If you tell me the complete and absolute truth, I will give you an antidote. But I want the truth." '

Schellenberg wondered if this was another of Heydrich's macabre jokes. As calmly as he could, he told Heydrich and Müller the details of the outing to Ploen.

Now Müller interrupted. 'After you had coffee, you went for a walk. Why didn't you admit that? You must have realized surely that you were being watched all the time.'

Schellenberg kept his temper. He realized that Müller had used Frau Heydrich's chauffeur to spy on him that afternoon. He told the other two the details of his quarter of an hour stroll with the Chief's wife, which must have satisfied Heydrich. For, after a few minutes of heavy silence, he said, 'Well, I suppose I have to believe you. But you'll give me your word of honour that you won't attempt this sort of thing again.'

Schellenberg was not appeased and said that Heydrich should give him the antidote to the supposed poison before he'd give his word of honour. Heydrich nodded and Schellenberg was given something that his boss called a dry Martini. Schellenberg thought it tasted very strongly of bitters. He drank it and asked permission to leave, which Heydrich refused, so they sat there drinking, with no more said about the incident.

It was a minor drunken interlude in the career of three ambitious secret policemen, a test of strength and power which such people are given to. But it was significant and a reflection yet again of the hold that Heydrich had over his subordinates. Now all three of them hated each other, but the two still continued to serve Heydrich until London finally put an end to his career.*

So the months passed. Dachau and other newer concentration camps opened by the new government started to fill

* See C. Whiting: *Heydrich: Henchman of Death* (Pen & Sword) for further details.

98

up with the victims of the brown terror. They were socialists, communists, 'Bible students' [Jehovah's Witnesses], homosexuals and other deviants, a whole cross-range of Germany, thousands and then hundreds of thousands of them. Before the Jews and foreigners throughout Occupied Europe were sent there, Dachau, Neuengamme, Mauthausen and the like were basically occupied by Germans. Unfortunately for the post-war Germany of our own time, after the war successive West German governments made no attempt to publicize this fact. To this very day the government of a now united Germany is paying, and paying heavily, for the lack of *Zivilcourage* in the post-war years.

The men who carried out these arrests back in the 1930s were no different. Many of them had political and religious convictions which they appeared to lose overnight. Socialists were persecuted by ex-Socialist policemen. Homosexuals among the ranks of the *Polizeiapparat* arrested fellow 'deviants' and slung them behind bars. Academics inside the universities who were paid police spies reported on their professorial colleagues and denounced them to the Gestapo. Although the Gestapo at this time numbered less than 1,000 officials, they appeared to the man-in-the-street to be everywhere. People grew afraid to speak on sensitive issues even to their closest friends because everyone knew the Gestapo were everywhere. Now before anyone said anything that might be misconstrued by the Gestapo spies known to be lurking in every shadow, he looked to left and right first. If the 'Heil Hitler' salute was known as the 'German Greeting', then that look became known as the 'German Look'; it was one of naked fear and apprehension.

Müller was no different from the rest. His main task was to apprehend communists; still, he helped in apprehending his fellow Bavarians who supported the priests in their Catholic faith or insisted on using the Bavarian *Grüss Gott* salutation instead of the new 'Heil Hitler'. Müller was surely exceeding the limits of his office, which was supposedly to deal exclusively with communist affairs, and, in particular, communist subversion.

As one of his colleagues, Doctor Wilhelm Hoettl, said of

him at that time, 'Müller was famous for his phenomenal memory. He could give at once and out of his head the name of some unimportant agent in a small town, and there was certainly no other police expert who possessed so wide a knowledge of personalities.'

According to Hoettl, this was the man who 'had perfected Heydrich's spy system by supervision. . . . Thanks to his activities the backbone of the German people was broken; not only did he stifle at birth any vestige of an opposition movement, but he maintained so rigorous and oppressive a grip on Party members that no one felt safe from the attentions of the Gestapo.' A harsh judgment indeed from a colleague.

But Hoettl went further. He maintained in his statement after the war that Müller wasn't concerned about the Party as such: 'The principles by which he judged men were not those upon which the judgments of the Party were based. The decisive factor, in his opinion, was whether the individual unreservedly and unconditionally obeyed the State, or whether he showed any tendency towards independent thought or action. He recognized no other law than that of the omnipotence of the State.'

Hoettl's judgment was typical of those made by all his other colleagues who put their thoughts on paper in statements which survived the war. No one seemed to understand him. No one liked him. So what was he up to? He was still not a Party member and even when he did become one he was smart enough to realize that the membership would never open any doors for him. The Party's politicos, the old guard at least, men like Hess and Goering, had long memories. They wouldn't forget the Müller of the old days in Munich. They would block any advancement that he sought.

2

THE YEARS OF POWER

'Ach, Schellenberg, after one has been in our profession for a while, one begins to see pink elephants everywhere.'

Abwehr Colonel Helfferich to SS General
Schellenberg, 1943.

1939: SPYMASTERS

'An intelligence service is the ideal vehicle for a conspiracy. Its members can travel about at home and abroad under secret orders and no questions asked.'

Allen Dulles, head of the American OSS in Switzerland, on the German Intelligence Service

ONE

As was his habit, the traitor slipped into Cologne's main station by the night train from Holland, some sixty miles away. Grasping his black briefcase, containing his samples and business cards which identified him as the Dutch agent for the Munich BMW firm, where decades before Müller had started his career as an apprentice aircraft fitter, he hurried across the square and slipped into the *Dom Hotel* in the shadow of the Rhenish capital's massive cathedral.

Hauptmann Giskes of the German Secret Service, *die Abwehr*, waited for him in the lobby. Giskes, long-nosed and foxy faced, was naturally in civilian clothes, but there still was no mistaking him for what he was – a former officer of the Imperial Army, recalled as a *Reserveoffizier der Grossdeutschen Wehrmacht.** Hands were shaken in the continental fashion. Coffee and cognac were drunk and the two men, spy and spymaster, got down to business.

As usual the spy, a naturalized Englishman who had been born Dutch, did most of the talking. Giskes let him talk, and talk the man did, but it was obvious to Giskes that the Dutchman's sources were running dry. By now, in the spring of 1939, most of the latter's contacts with the British Continental Secret Intelligence Service in Holland were

---

* Giskes had been brought into the *Abwehr* two years before by his chief, Captain von Feldmann, who told him he shouldn't let himself 'be shot to pieces for Hitler' by rejoining his old artillery unit.

105

gone. All the same Giskes suspected that the Dutchman still had something in reserve. As he recalled* many years later, I realized he had an ace up his sleeve, one vital last card. And I was determined to get it by hook or by crook.'

Now he played his own card. With an air of finality he said, 'Let me know when we can meet again, when you get some more information.'

The Dutch traitor looked crestfallen. 'But when?' he asked.

Giskes shrugged. 'Your stuff is not interesting enough for me to come all this way from Hamburg to meet you.'

An awkward silence followed. Giskes confessed later, 'I was worried I'd overdone it. After all he was the only agent I had.'

The traitor hesitated. 'I know a man,' he said somewhat uncertainly. 'But if I tell you his name, you'll hang him.' He looked appealingly at Giskes, as if he wanted confirmation that he wouldn't.

'I can't guarantee it, but I promise you that I'll do my best to save him,' Giskes reassured him.

The traitor was still reluctant to give any more details, but he said he'd need money for the information. As always he was broke again. 'How much do you want?' When the traitor wouldn't come up with a figure, the German snapped, 'All right, I'll give you five thousand guilders if your information is important.'

The other still hesitated. 'I can't tell you his name.'

Giskes was no longer playing. Harshly he said, tossing a pencil onto the table, 'All right then, *write* it.'

'His name is Krueger,' the traitor whispered.

'There are thousands of Kruegers in Germany,' Giskes objected. 'I'll want more details than that.' He slapped a wad of notes on the table. That did it.

'His name is Krueger, Otto Krueger. The British call him Doctor Krueger. He lives in Bad Godesberg near Bonn. But he comes to Holland for his meetings with the station head.' He meant the local chief of the Continental British Secret Intelligence Service. 'He stays at the Amstel in Amsterdam or

* To the author.

106

in the Hotel des Indes at the Hague.' Both were, and are, expensive places and Giskes knew that the British must have valued his services highly to spend that kind of money on him.

Thus, in the elegant comfort of Cologne's best hotel, the traitor betrayed the identity of Britain's second most important super-spy, whose code number was still classified long after the war (it was 33016).*

A few minutes later the two men parted. It would be another six years before John Hooper, the naturalized British traitor, and Giskes would meet again in a secret SIS internment and interrogation camp outside London. By then their lives would have changed dramatically. But that day in 1939 Giskes still had a long career in espionage ahead of him.† He caught the train back to Hamburg to report to his Intelligence bosses. 'They were aghast in Hamburg when I told them about Krueger,' Giskes recalled long afterwards. 'Some of them even knew him personally. It turned out that Doctor Krueger had been an engineer lieutenant in the old Imperial Navy. After being demobilized he had been recruited by the British Secret Intelligence Service to keep an eye on his old comrades in the post-war *Kriegsmarine*, the German Navy.'

Krueger had prospered with British money and through his own talents. He had been awarded an honorary doctorate and in the mid-thirties he had been elected a director of the very important Federation of German Industry (*Industrieverband*). Naturally these connections provided him with excellent sources of information, in addition to what he obtained from his naval friends about German marine rearmament. Thus Dr Krueger had been able to lead a double life with his SIS payments camouflaged as returns from his inventions patented in the UK.

Now the *Abwehr* in Hamburg, which had no power of arrest, turned the case over to the Gestapo, and Heydrich, as an ex-naval officer himself, was particularly interested. He

* Winterbotham, the guardian of the 'Ultra Secret', still remembered the number forty-odd years later when he revealed it to the author: it demonstrates how important Krueger had been.
† See C. Whiting: *Hitler's Secret War* (Pen & Sword) for further details.

put Müller in overall charge and for the first time the Bavarian entered the world of espionage, that dirty war in the shadows which would be his major concern throughout the six years of total war soon to come.

Müller went through the usual routine checks, trying to find some link between Krueger's treachery and his private circumstances. His mail, phone, bank account and private life were screened. Nothing! He wasn't a homosexual and thereby open to blackmail, as was often the case in those days, and he wasn't betraying his wife with a mistress. Everything was perfectly above board. Müller concluded that Krueger just liked spying for the *frisson* it gave him.

Finally the *Abwehr* gave him the evidence he needed for an arrest. Krueger and his wife were spotted visiting a lonely villa outside the Hague suburb of Scheveningen after midnight one night during a seemingly harmless visit to Holland. Admiral Canaris made enquiries. He discovered that the villa belonged to a Herr August de Fremery, who it turned out, was, in reality, Captain Hendricks, the deputy head of the SIS in the Hague.

On 7 July 1939 Otto Krueger, Agent 33016, was arrested by Müller's men in Hamburg. There he was kept for prolonged 'severe interrogation' in the city's *Stadtgefängnis* (Town Prison). One day after Britain declared war on Germany its long-term agent committed suicide.

Müller had had his first taste of espionage. Now he was selected to discover the identity of a spy who was really a very big fish. Indeed he would turn out to be a personal friend of Himmler. But with the imminent approach of the new war, Müller had other and more pressing fish to fry. He had to help start the Second World War Two.

On 15 August 1939 Alfred Naujocks, an ex-student of engineering, stepped up to the entrance to the Security Police HQ at No 10 Prinz Albrecht Platz. Once it had been a girls' college; now it was the most feared building in Central Berlin. For it was the headquarters of the Gestapo, where Heydrich, Müller, Nebe and Schellenberg held sway.

The guards clicked to attention. Naujocks, who had been called back from the Polish-German frontier that hot summer's day, nodded and passed into the cool of the interior. He went on to the Chief's office and was surprised to find two other very important officers waiting there in full fig: Müller and Arthur Nebe, head of the *Kripo*. Naujocks liked neither of them, but then they didn't like him. He was an upstart, a Nazi bullyboy, not a trained policeman with years of experience like they were. Nevertheless they returned the younger officer's 'Heil Hitler'. After all Naujocks was a special protégé of the Chief.

For a while Heydrich paced up and down nervously, as if he hesitated to speak. Finally he said, 'I have asked you to come here to discuss the execution of an order which has come from the Führer himself. We are concerned with a matter that goes far beyond anything we have done before.'

He let them absorb the information. Then he got down to business. 'We are concerned with a mission which will attract worldwide attention. For it we will need two hundred men. That means there will be two hundred people *in the know*.' He looked hard at Naujocks, who knew what that look meant. Anyone who opened his mouth about this affair would die a sudden death.

Now Heydrich turned to Müller. 'You will provide at least fifty people from the concentration camps.'

The latter nodded. The people he would select would be as good as dead as soon as he had selected them. In the event they'd be dead *before* the mission actually took place.

Heydrich confirmed his thinking the next moment. 'As dead people only can keep their trap shut . . .' He didn't complete his sentence.

'What about the others?' Naujocks asked. He had been on such missions before and felt entitled to speak.

'I'll pick them, Naujocks. The best men available. Real men who are scared of nothing.'

Naujocks realized that this was to be a major op. After all three SS generals were involved. Still he refrained from asking the obvious question and contented himself with, 'How are we going to keep the operation secret?'

Instead of answering his question, Heydrich asked one of his own: 'What would you do?'

Naujocks was caught off guard. 'Subject them to a special oath.' Even as he said the words, he knew they were foolish. Only dead men couldn't talk. Heydrich would have them killed as the best form of secrecy. Would the Chief have *him* liquidated too?

'We can't take that risk,' Heydrich said with a shake of his head. 'But nobody will harm them. Afterwards they will be given plenty of opportunities to sacrifice themselves for Folk, Fatherland and Führer.' Mockingly he used the standard Nazi phrase of that year. 'They will be allowed to die a soldier's death at the front.'

A sudden silence fell on the office. According to his own account, Naujocks broke the hush with 'At the front?' He looked puzzled. Front meant war.

Heydrich nodded calmly. 'Yes at the front. There's going to be a war and we, gentlemen, are going to start it, with the men we will select tomorrow morning.'

Later the cynical operation which Germany used as an excuse for the Nazis' attack on Poland was recorded in history as the 'Gleiwitz Incident'. It was a feigned Polish attack on the German border radio station at the little Silesian town of that name. The Incident, of which all the main participants were dead or vanished by the time the war was over, is a puzzle to this day. But Müller's part in it is relatively straightforward and began with the procurement of the 'canned goods'.*

Over the next few days, while Europe teetered on the edge of war, Naujocks, who was going to lead the 'Polish' attack on the Gleiwitz Radio Station, conferred with Müller a couple of times about these strangely named 'canned goods'. He discovered that Müller was to select a number of young male German prisoners from the concentration camps, some of whom would be able to speak Polish. They would be dressed in Polish uniforms and given Polish weapons. On the

---

* Naujocks wisely deserted to the British in Belgium in October 1944. They arrested him, but he seems to have disappeared again between then and the end of the war to reappear in the early '50s as a bouncer in Hamburg's red-light district where he sold his 'memoires' repeatedly to journalists for the price of a few drinks.

appointed day they would masquerade as Polish irregulars attacking the radio station. But why the strange name of the op?

Müller smiled. He had dangled a carrot in front of the concentration camp inmates; if they weren't shot in the initial rush, they would be rewarded with their immediate freedom. That obviously wouldn't be the case. They'd be returned to their camps and quietly 'dispensed with'.*

Then Müller told Naujocks that two minutes after the latter began the attack with his 'Poles', he, Müller, would drive up to the radio station in a black Opel and deposit a body, freshly killed and dressed in Polish uniform, on the steps. Thereafter his part in the operation would be ended.

'Don't lose any sleep over the victim,' Müller told him. 'He's been chosen already – from a Jewish concentration camp. And for your information I have christened this part of the affair *"Unternehmen Konserven"* (Canned Goods). Now Naujocks knew the reason for the name. Müller was going to deliver a cargo of dead men (there'd be more than just the one on the steps) for the operation which would spark off the Second World War. Indeed he was taking a macabre delight in this new cloak-and-dagger existence into which he was being initiated. All the same, cautious peasant that he was, Müller wasn't going to risk his own neck. After his part was completed, he was determined to get out of harm's way. He was evidently not interested in the honours that would be heaped on the others when the operation was over.

On the morning of Friday 1 September 1939 Hitler's own paper, the *Völkische Beobachter*, bore a banner headline screeching, 'POLISH INSURGENTS CROSS THE GERMAN FRONTIER'! The editorial went on to explain that the 'Gleiwitz crime' was clearly the signal 'for a general attack on German territory by Polish guerrillas'. A few hours later Hitler called

---

* One of the 'canned goods' actually did survive. He got back to his camp, feigned a sudden illness, was overlooked in the excitement of the new war and forgotten. When he was finally released, he immediately joined the Army and managed to survive the war and testify to the truth of this bold if cruel operation.

a session of the rubber-stamp parliament, the *Reichstag*, and thundered, 'Since four-forty-five this morning our cannon have been firing back!' The Third Reich was at war with Poland. The tragedy had begun.

Immediately after the 'Incident' the world's press rushed to Gleiwitz in Upper Silesia, while column after column of soldiers marched eastwards to their eventual death. They wanted to see the scene of 'that dastardly Polish provocation', as the German media called it. There, waiting for them, was SS *Gruppenführer* Müller in his new SS General's uniform. He was in charge of the 'investigation'. If anyone could find out the truth, it would be him.

He lectured the pressmen with the aid of a model of the radio station at Gleiwitz, accurate down to the smallest detail. Naturally – for it was the same model that he and the rest of the plotters had used to train the 'Polish insurgents'!

In the background, the Chief paced back and forth as he listened to Müller explain his suspicions in his broad Bavarian dialect. At intervals Heydrich would nod his head sagely. Now and again one of the pressmen would hear him declare, as if speaking to himself, 'Yes, yes, that's how it started.'

TWO

On Wednesday, March 15 1939, when the London *Daily Mail* headlined the news of the German takeover of Czechoslovakia, it also carried another story. Above a picture of three Czech Intelligence men peering out of the window of the plane which had brought them the night before from Prague to Croydon, the headline reads 'Eleven Mystery Men Arrive by Air. Sign Secret Register.' That day a certain Dr Paul Hans Steinberg registered at the Hotel Golden Goose in Prague's Wenzelplatz Square. He was known by a code number to those men now in London. It was 'A-54' and the German, using the name Steinberg, who had now spied for them for the last three years, had come to the former Czech capital to spy for another intelligence organization, the German *Abwehr*. Meanwhile the eleven Czechs, who had been taken over by the British SIS, waited in their temporary quarters at the Grosvenor Hotel for 'A-54's' next move. Their country no longer existed. They, the former spymasters, (and paymasters, too, it must be pointed out) were no longer in charge. Would the victor still be willing to work for the vanquished? He would.

On 13 April 1939 Lieutenant Alois Frank of Czech Intelligence, who had first recruited this mysterious German agent (after three years the Czechs still did not know his real name), received a postcard with a message written on it under the usual greetings – in milk! 'It confirmed that 'A-54' was still prepared to work for them.

Now, as the war began, the German agent's messages from Prague and from Saxony in Germany proved a godsend. At that time British Intelligence knew virtually nothing about what was happening in 'Twelveland', their codename for Germany. All its agents in that country had been wiped out and their overflights of German territory had become too dangerous. 'A-54', who seemed to have friends in very high places, was Britain's only source of accurate information about German intentions. Ultra was not yet functioning correctly and the Czechs, a small exiled group with no resources, not even a budget, were playing a disproportionate role, in view of their position, in British affairs.

But the mysterious German agent came up with the goods. He revealed to the Czechs and their British masters in Queen Anne's Gate, HQ of the SIS, the German invasion plan for France (the French General Staff refused to believe it). Later he informed London that Hitler had called off 'Operation Sea Lion', the invasion of the UK. Churchill was very relieved to hear that, but, for political reasons, he kept the news secret; and, although Station X, the Bletchley listening post, already knew about Hitler's next intention, 'A-54' also revealed that Germany was going to attack Soviet Russia.

As Dr Benes, the Czech President-in-Exile in London, recorded in his memoirs: 'From the beginning of 1940, we received daily information from an absolutely unimpeachable source in Prague and Berlin.' Naturally the source was 'A-54', alias Dr Steinberg, alias Dr Holm, alias Jochen Breitner, and all the other names the spy gave himself, not only to fool the Gestapo, but also his Czech contacts.

But who was he in reality? His real name was Paul Thuemmel, a baker by trade, born in 1902 in Neuhausen on the German side of the Erzgebirge Mountains. At the age of 25 he had started the local branch of the Nazi Party. To celebrate the event he had invited a relatively unimportant member of Hitler's party to his remote provincial town to speak to his new members. His name was Heinrich Himmler, one day to be Müller's boss.

Himmler stayed the night, slept in the baker's house

and was much taken by the kindness of the hostess, Frau Thuemmel, the future spy's mother, who made a great fuss of him. Soon they were addressing each other with the familiar 'thou' and when Thuemmel went to Bavaria on Party business Himmler was often his host. Thereafter, they continued to correspond, almost to the end.

In 1933, after the Nazi Party's takeover, Himmler got his friend a post with the Saxon branch of the German military secret service, The *Abwehr*. It did not then have many Nazis among its ranks and perhaps Himmler used Thuemmel to spy upon the suspect Army organization. But in Dresden, where Thuemmel would serve for three years, he was prepared to spy, but not for Himmler. Instead he offered his services to Czechs for money. He told his Czech spymasters that he spied for them because he was of Slavic blood, not a particularly good recommendation as Slavs were regarded as third-class citizens.

It is difficult to understand why he continued to spy for the Czechs after that nation disappeared. Did the Czechs black-mail him? Or did he, as an old SA man, hate the SS on account of what they had done to his old outfit during the Night of the Long Knives? We don't know. But we do know that by 1940 the British were rating him as their top agent, due to the fact that, among other things, he could confirm the Bletchley Ultra decodes and had warned them of the Duke of Windsor's contacts with the Nazis and that Schellenberg had hatched some sort of plan to kidnap him in Lisbon.

But by then the Gestapo were trying to find 'A-54'. For a long time Müller's agents had been trying to trace the illegal radio stations in Prague, which they knew were in contact with London. Time and again they failed. Once one of Müller's men, Commissar Fleischer, just missed the head of the Czech radio game. Thereafter the man in question smuggled himself into the Prague Gestapo Headquarters and cheekily wrote on a wall: 'I was waiting for you, Fleischer. Where were you?' That bold trick should have alerted Müller to the fact that there was something suspect about his own officials in Prague. How could a member of the enemy underground get in and scrawl messages of that kind and still get away with it?

On 3 October, however, three months after Germany had invaded Russia and the Czech state had become vital to Germany's new war in the East (in the end the Czechs in the Skoda plants were manufacturing a quarter of all the Wehrmacht's armoured vehicles used to fight the Russians), Fleischer struck lucky. He and his team captured the key Czech radio centre transmitting to London. With it was found a hoard of high-grade material, which indicated that there was a traitor, presumably right at the top of the Nazi state and a German to boot!

Along the whole Gestapo network from Prague through East Germany to the Berlin Prinz Albrecht HQ the alarm bells started to ring. At a certain level Heydrich and his men were feared and all powerful. But as far as the Führer was concerned they were basically state officials working in a police capacity, and Heydrich knew and feared the Führer's temper. Only a few months before two of his old SD officials, working for counter-espionage from Breslau, had disappeared and turned up in Russia with a suitcase full of classified Gestapo material. Now there seemed to be an even bigger fish in their midst.

Heydrich acted immediately and decisively, although, at that time, among his other many duties, he was secretly flying combat missions against the Russians.* He formed the 'Verraeter X' (Traitor X) Team, a special Gestapo search squad, directly under Müller's control, to find the traitor. They knew that he lived somewhere to the north of Prague, but so did two hundred thousand other civilians. Where to start?

But the 'Traitor X Team' had two special Gestapo men working for it, Commissar Willi Leimar and Commissar Nachtmann. These two had succeeded in worming their way

---

* The mind boggles at the thought of the man who knew the secrets that Heydrich did being allowed to fly deep into enemy territory. Indeed, Heydrich was once shot down and survived a two-day struggle to return to his own lines!

116

into the Czech underground and were now busy betraying the Czechs to their own organization. Were they just honest German cops doing their job? No, they were triple traitors. For both the Gestapo men, old pre-Nazi-period veterans, were long-time agents of the Soviet Secret Service, the NKVD. For that organization was determined to destroy the Czech resistance which reported to Benes and his right-wing reactionaries in London.

Understandably both commissars were regarded as 'Red experts' in Berlin, just as Müller was. Indeed, the latter took particular interest in the careers of the two commissars and, despite their low rank, gave them personal orders.

On Müller's specific instructions the two arrested a Czech communist in the Prague suburb of Karlin. His name was Antonin Novotny. He was sent to the concentration camp at Mauthausen where he waxed exceedingly fat as a *Kapo*, while another obscure Czech communist named Stefan Dubcek waned exceedingly thin. Both would survive Mauthausen and the war and go on to gain international fame in the '60s. Müller's motives, in the light of what was to be written about him in that same decade, still remain obscure.

But now Nachtmann and Leimer were working all out for the Russians. 'Konsul', the Russian spy resident in Prague, ordered them to break the Czech resistance movement and their mainstay, Paul Thuemmel.

Indirectly Thuemmel was known to the two men. After the French General Staff had taken no notice of 'A-54's' warning that the Germans were going to attack France the year before, he had begun to distrust his case officers, Czech and British, in London. As a result he had made a preliminary approach to the Russians through the Czech resistance. It had been a fatal move. The Czechs passed his name on to the two supposed fellow resistance workers, Nachtmann and Leimer.

Now, with the heat on from Berlin, and presumably from their Russian spymaster Konsul, the two Gestapo men informed the 'Traitor X' squad. So it was that Thuemmel was finally arrested on 13 October 1941.

As for Nachtmann and Leimer, they passed out of the

picture and continued their treacherous activities right up to the time that the Gestapo had finally to flee Prague.*

Naturally the Gestapo grilled Himmler's friend discreetly but intensively. An old-time cop, Willi Abendschoen, who two years before had worked on the captured British SIS chiefs Best and Stevens with Müller, was put on the case. Willi was no Gestapo brute as portrayed in the Hollywood movies. Now and again he'd give a suspect a slap or a cuff, but then all Continental, and American, cops did that. But he worked subtly, using statements and contradictory statements to trap the prisoner, make him tell the truth and confess of his own volition and, in the end, Abendschoen succeeded.

For Abendschoen caught him out on one important point, connected with his last important case, the interrogation of the two captured SIS officers. The slow-talking Gestapo man recalled that during the interrogation of the agents, captured by Naujocks and Schellenberg at Venlo on the German-Dutch frontier, they had mentioned a high-ranking German. This German had come to visit them at their HQ in the Hague in 1939.

Abendschoen checked. He discovered that in that year Thuemmel had stopped at the *Abwehr* office in Münster on his way to the Hague. It was his only break in his journey to meet the Czechs, who had fled to London. That did it. Thuemmel started to blab. But what to do with him? After all he was Himmler's friend. What a scandal it would be if it was discovered that the head of the Gestapo had had a long-term relationship with such a high-ranking traitor.

Müller, who must have been chuckling up his sleeve at the

* In 1944, for instance, a Czech SOE agent working as a secretary for the Prague Gestapo warned London that the local resistance was in danger. The Czech resistance head informed his most trusted man, a 'Lieutenant Sulc'. In turn 'Sulc' betrayed the brave SOE female agent to the Gestapo. 'Sulc' was Commissar Nachtmann. Major Frolik, a post-war Czech defector, told the author that in 1962, during his own enquiries into the Thuemmel Affair, he was informed by the Russians that their files on the two Gestapo agents had been burned in 1950. A colleague informed him that wasn't true. One at least was still working for the Russians as a colonel in the Moscow HQ of the KGB!

whole business, made a suggestion to Himmler, which was taken up. A few days later 'A-54' was given the last of his many aliases. As Major Peter Toman, the 'former Dutch military attaché' in Prague, he was delivered into Theresienstadt Concentration camp, where the guards were surprised that he didn't seem to speak a word of his 'native' language, Dutch, and thus passes out of our story. *

But the arrest of Thuemmel and the realization that there were traitors at the highest level set some of the Nazi *Prominenz* thinking. Walter Schellenberg, now an SS colonel and soon to be a general, was one. Naturally he couldn't know about Nachtmann's and Leimar's treachery, but he felt all was not right within the ranks of the Gestapo itself. For now, with Gestapo officials roaming the length of Occupied Europe and because of their lack of numbers being forced to use foreigners as agents, informers and spies, corruption was becoming ever more evident in the organization.

In particular, the young ex-lawyer began to focus his attention more and more on Müller, who was developing 'elbows', as the Germans put it. He was becoming aggressive in his demands; indeed he had even suggested to the Chief that there should be a complete reorganization of the Gestapo and the SD, with the two key SS organizations perhaps being amalgamated. To assist him, he had recruited Hitler's 'Brown Eminence' Martin Bormann into his camp.

As Schellenberg recorded: 'Müller realized that Bormann would become Hess's successor [after Hess's flight to Scotland] and that he was a personality of much greater dynamic force. Privately Müller established good relations with Bormann while pretending to oppose him strongly, as far as Himmler and Heydrich were concerned. It still seems strange to me that Heydrich did not see through the game that Müller was playing, a game which was later to become of considerable importance.'

But Heydrich continued to poo-pooh Schellenberg's fears, saying that Müller was a 'simple Bavarian peasant'. On one

* 'A-54' survived till 20 April 1945, Hitler's birthday, when he passed through the camp's 'door of death' to be executed by firing squad.

occasion, for instance, he even criticized him in front of Schellenberg after a lot of drink at Berlin's posh Eden Bar. Müller had just accused Schellenberg of bad judgment. Heydrich had responded with a cutting, 'I'm sure misadventures of this sort have also happened in your department, Müller. For instance when an important witness is given the opportunity to throw himself out of a fourth-floor window, not only because your investigators are asleep on the job, but because they haven't even mastered the ABC of police procedure.' That must have hurt and, as a gleeful Schellenberg recalled, 'This time Müller had really burned his fingers and, for three or four weeks I was left in peace.'

But soon Schellenberg's protector would be dead. Then he and anyone who got in Müller's way would have reason to rue ever meeting that 'simple Bavarian peasant'.

1. At a wartime concert in Norway: 1. Vidkun Quisling; 2. Gauleiter Terboven; 3. General von Falkenhorst; 4. "Gestapo" Müller.

2. Members of the Nazi hierarchy: 1. Walter Schellenberg; 2. Müller; 3. Reinhard Heydrich.

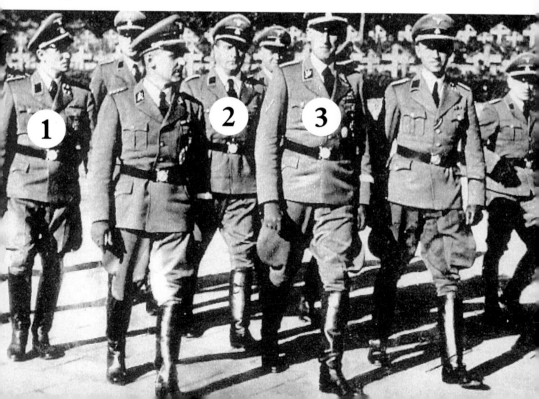

3. 1. Artur Nebe; 2. Heinrich Himmler; 3. Heydrich; 4. Müller.

4. 1. Mussolini; 2. Martin Bormann; 3. Admiral Dönitz; 4. Hitler; 5. Hermann
   Goering; 6. General Fegelein.

5. Ernst Roehm, notorious homosexual and head of the SA.

6. The author outside the Bürgerbräu in Munich where it all started in 1923.

7. The Stadelheim Prison where Müller had Roehm locked up and where, some thirty years later, the two Mossad agents, Schur and Gordon, were imprisoned.

8. Cell No. 7 in the Stadelheim Prison where Roehm was shot in 1934.

9. Reinhard Heydrich makes the cover of *Time* magazine in 1942.

10. The "Salon Kitty" in 1939, the Berlin brothel which Heydrich set up for the Nazi top brass.

11. The Berghof, Hitler's retreat in the Bavarian Alps.

12. Hitler chooses a wedding present for General Fegelein, who married the sister of Eva Braun, Hitler's mistress. Behind him is Martin Bormann.

13. The author with Putzi Hanfstaengl.

14. Heydrich's daughter in the restaurant which her father bought before the war.

15. Heydrich's widow shows the author the plate given to her son by Roehm as a christening present.

17. The end in Berlin. A dead SS man lies in front of the Brandenburg Gate.

16. Kempka, Hitler's driver, who led one of the escape groups from the Bunker in May, 1945.

18. The stone which marks the burial place of "Gestapo" Müller – or not?

THREE

Six weeks after Thuemmel was sent to the concentration camp under his last alias, Reinhard Heydrich summoned a conference of his own senior officers, including Müller and Admiral Canaris of the *Abwehr*. Naturally the intelligence community had been badly shocked by the discovery of the traitor in their midst, but Heydrich and Müller had come out of it well, whereas Canaris had failed to discover that Thuemmel had been a member of his own organization. Not only the Gestapo's extended operations were lax in their new European role, but obviously the *Abwehr*'s were too. The time had come, in effect, to amalgamate all the Reich's intelligence communities. Naturally they'd be under Heydrich's command. Müller's plan was beginning to unfold.

At 10.30 am on May 18 Heydrich and Canaris appeared at the Prague HQ and the keynote conference began. Heydrich naturally made the opening speech. He was followed by Canaris, who suggested, without apparently realizing the underlying purpose of the conference, that there should, indeed, be closer cooperation between his organization and the SD and Gestapo.

The third speaker was Müller. Once Captain Best of the SIS had described him as 'a decent little man', after the latter had interrogated him several times in the cellars of the Prinz Albrecht HQ. Now he was no longer so 'decent'. He made no attempt to conceal his contempt for the *Abwehr*. He said that

121

the Admiral's organization was old-fashioned and incompetent. There had been grave mistakes made. Now there had to be changes, drastic changes.

Heydrich summed up the conference's findings. He stated categorically that if the *Abwehr* and his organization were to work together in their future, Canaris would have to agree to what he called the 'Heydrich Decalogue' (or the 'Ten Commandments of the Prague God', as Müller called them when Heydrich was out of earshot). These were harsh and brutal. 'Because of the situation at home and abroad,' he stated, the organization and personnel of the *Abwehr* must be changed. 'The present officers of the *Abwehr* have shown themselves incapable and must be replaced by men trained by the SS. In the interests of Reich Security there must be a centralized secret service organization. Its representatives must be empowered to act in all departments and to draw on total manpower. These men are to be responsible to their Minister, the Minister of State, *and to me!*' Heydrich sought total control, and when he had it, his most senior officer, the new SS General Heinrich Müller, responsible for the day-to-day working of the new organization, would have it too.

But there was a major hiccup on the way. Nine days after that Prague conference Reinhard Heydrich was fatally wounded by the two Czech SOE agents, Gabcik and Kubis, parachuted into their native country to carry out the controversial assassination. Eight days later Heydrich died.

On the day that Heydrich died the Germans, on Hitler's express order, gave an ultimatum to the Czechs. If they didn't deliver Heydrich's killers to the German authorities by 16 June 1942 they would suffer a terrible fate. On that same day the *Wehrmacht* and Gestapo made their first reconnaissance of Lidice village, a name which would be soon known around the world. On 9 June at a quarter to eight in the evening the Germans went into action. All the village males were to be shot, all females sent to a concentration camp and those children who could be 'aryanized', on account of their 'Germanic' appearance were to be put up for adoption in German families. The rest would naturally die with the adults.

Now the plotters knew that the Germans weren't fooling. One of them, another paratrooper trained in the UK, Karel Curda, broke. He accepted the huge reward that the Gestapo had offered for the killers of their feared boss. Curda was brought up in front of one of Müller's old cops, *Ober-kommissar* Heinz Pannwitz. The latter soon had the Czech agent 'singing like a canary'. Of Pannwitz it was said in Gestapo HQ, 'He can make even a mummy talk'.

Curda began to give away names, especially those of the Czech resistance who had hidden the killers and those who were perhaps still hiding them. They were arrested. Without waiting for Himmler's permission, the Gestapo started to torture their captives in the cellars of Prague's Pecek Palais. One who refused to talk, for instance, was confronted with the severed head of his mother brought in in a fish tank! He talked.

Within hours the Gestapo knew where the killers and their associates in the Czech resistance were hiding – in the catacombs of the St Cyril and Methodius Church in Central Prague. What were the Germans to do? They needed the Czechs to continue working for them in the war industries. The war in Russia wasn't going well, as it was, and the last thing they wanted was a Czech workers' strike. So if they shot the men hiding in the cellars out of hand – they were after all regarded by their fellows as patriots – they risked serious problems with the work force. At the same time, however, the Führer wanted revenge. He demanded the heads of the Czech killers if they weren't prepared to surrender.

Himmler, who seemed to be glad that Heydrich was dead – he told *Obergruppenführer* Oswald Pohl, 'You know that I have taken over as Leader of the Security Services in succession to Heydrich' – kept his nose out of the business and Müller appears to have been left in charge. He went to work on the Czech plotters with remarkable energy. In essence, he appeared to be simply carrying out the Führer's orders. It seemed that he didn't want a show trial, which would reveal

123

that the Czechs were paid assassins who had murdered Heydrich, the known 'benefactor' of the Czech people*, on the orders of the British.

Instead, seven hundred SS troops under the command of SS General von Treuenfeld, plus the Gestapo, Czech police and fire-brigade, were alerted for an attack on the Czechs hiding in the catacombs. The assault turned into a sorry mess. The Czechs might be heavily outnumbered, but the SS could only attack in small numbers and on a limited front. Three lone Czechs, for instance, held off the battalion-sized SS troopers for two hours. Poison gas was pumped in. Still the Czechs kept up their heroic defence. Pannwitz, in charge, was pulling out his hair by now. He and Curda and another captured Czech brought into the debris-littered church, the crypt of which was now being flooded by the Czech fire brigade as another means of trying to force the defenders out.

'Surrender, boys,' Curda called to them on German orders, 'everything will be all right.'

His answer was a burst of Sten-gun fire.

Von Treuenfeld and the local Party Boss Karl Frank were getting impatient. The honour of the SS was at stake. Pannwitz, who wanted prisoners, was told, 'What does the Gestapo know of war? Why should these damned Czechs be taken alive?'

Frank agreed, although a harassed Pannwitz assured him that he needed a mere six hours to get the remaining Czechs to surrender. But the two senior officers weren't listening to the civilian any longer.

Now, according to von Treuenfeld, a brief firefight took place. Other reports maintain that even before the firefight the inevitable happened. Four shots echoed from the crypt below. A man was sent to find out what had happened. '*Fertig*,' he shouted back. The Czechs were finished.

As von Treuenfeld wrote in his report, 'Four dead criminals

---

* In order to keep the Czech workforce happy, Heydrich had introduced the German system of social security – sick pay, paid holidays and extra heavy-worker rations.

were found in the crypt. Apart from serious injuries, they had wounds in their temples, showing they had killed themselves with their own revolvers.'

At the moment the SS started to drag out the dead bodies to pose with them on the street above, a messenger arrived from Himmler. The message he brought read: 'Any means should be employed to reassure the assassins in order to capture them alive.' Pannwitz shrugged, as he read it aloud to Frank; the latter had forgotten his glasses. What did it matter now? But it was strange that Himmler had suddenly become so concerned about the fate of the murderers.

But if the British had really sent the Czech SOE men in to kill Heydrich in the hope there would be large-scale German reprisals, resulting in reduced Czech armamant production, they were to be disappointed. Instead production increased. The SOE calculated that sixty-five percent of the Czech population were actively cooperating with the Germans (Polish Intelligence put it as high as eighty percent). Skoda, the mainstay of Czech armament production, outdid itself. It produced most of the *Wehrmacht*'s cannon and self-propelled guns. Ironically enough, many of the guns that fired on the Allied liberators on D-Day in France were produced by Occupied Czechoslovakia (Slovakia itself had joined the German camp and provided four divisions for the Russian front).

Death had come to the tyrant all right. But seemingly it hadn't changed the nature of the war one iota, save in one minor detail. Heydrich's plans to centralize the various German security and secret service organizations had come to nothing. Admiral Canaris would continue to run his *Abwehr* independently for another two years before he was arrested.* In a way the Admiral benefited from Heydrich's death.

It is a point that some writers on Heydrich have seized upon. They maintain that, on the surface, Heydrich was assassinated to *force* the Germans into taking reprisals. These reprisals would, in turn, create such a hatred in the Czechs

* See Whiting: *Hitler's Secret War* for further details.

that they would refuse to work for the German war industry.

There could be some truth in this argument, save that the Czechs didn't want Heydrich assassinated or any other of the targets originally suggested by their government in London. Benes, in the British capital, appears to have understood his readers' point-of-view and it did take the para-killers six months after they had been dropped until they finally carried out their attack. Benes' explanation was that he was being pressured by the British government to assassinate Heydrich and was drawing the matter out as long as possible. But there is clear evidence that the British Government was not involved in the planning of the attack and that the proposal was never placed before the Allied Joint Intelligence Committee, which dealt with all such matters. So who ordered Heydrich killed and why?

We do know that the SIS played a major role in planning the assassination. Colonel Wilson of the SIS trained the Czechs in Northern Scotland and it was SIS officers who provided the Canadian crew and Halifax bomber which took the Czechs to their date with destiny. Since that time the SIS have made it difficult for researchers into the Heydrich killing to rattle that 'well-stocked morgue of bones for historians', as one of the first writers on the subject has put it.*

Could it have been Menzies, head of the SIS, who was really behind the murder? Did he plan the Heydrich assassination because he wanted to protect his organization's treacherous connections with Canaris' *Abwehr*? With Heydrich out of the way, the *Abwehr* would be able to continue its contacts with the British secret service unhindered until, in 1943, Müller start to crack down on those *Abwehr* agents who were flirting with the enemy in Turkey, Switzerland, Sweden and elsewhere. But if that were the case, it would have seemingly gone against SIS policy. Throughout the war Menzies never allowed his operatives to take part in a political assassination such as that of Heydrich. Time and again, even before the start of the war, senior men in his organization had proposed an attempt on Hitler's life,

---

* Alan Burgess: *Seven Men at Daybreak*, Evans Bros.

but it never came to pass. Throughout the six years of the war, Reinhard Heydrich was the only senior German figure to be assassinated.

So if the Czech agents didn't do it on Menzies' orders, who was behind this unique political murder? And why, when it would have been to Germany's advantage to hold a major show trial (they kept Thuemmel alive for *three more years* because they wanted him as chief witness in a court room drama they were going to stage in London after they had won the war) did they kill the Czechs in the crypt so swiftly? After all, the killers and their helpers would have been much more important as witnesses than Thuemmel. Indeed, in retrospect, it looks as if the Gestapo wanted the whole affair hushed up as quickly as possible. Yet politically it would have been to the German advantage to do the contrary.

Russia, as is now known, was very active in Czechoslovakia. Ever since Germany's attack on Russia, Czechoslovakia had been the number one target for Russia's intelligence services. They had their fingers in every pie, with parachute agents being dropped all over the eastern part of the country.

Moscow had two primary targets. One was the same as that of Britain: the reduction of Czech war production for the German forces. The other was a specifically Russian objective. It was the destruction of the major Czech resistance organization which was taking its orders from the exiled Czech government. Discredit these and the underground Czech communist party, small but very powerful, would have a free hand.

But there was perhaps another objective which Russia pursued and which, surprisingly enough, could only be achieved if the Germans assisted them. It was to make the Germans bury Heydrich quickly and forget the whole business.

We know from Schellenberg that Heydrich's death caused consternation in Prinz Albrecht Strasse: 'The assassination certainly had its effect on the work of the central office in Berlin. Instead of the hum of intensive activity, there was a hush of incredulity, almost of fear. How could such a thing have happened?'

A hush of fear? Certainly. Could they be next, the high-ranking security men in charge of Occupied Europe must have asked themselves. In the event they were safe. Only one more political assassination was attempted in the occupied territories, the low-level murder of *Gauleiter* Erich Kuby by partisans in the East. Instead, it seems, the death of Heydrich signalled the start of what would become a rush of those in the security services now desirous of saving their hides by talking with the Western Allies.

Admiral Canaris might have broken down at Heydrich's funeral and told Schellenberg that 'Heydrich was a great man. I have lost a friend in him.' Six months later he was in Spain hoping to meet 'C', the head of SIS.* Schellenberg was no different. Within the year he had attached himself to a new patron, Himmler, and would soon start, with his boss, making his first approaches, mainly through 'natural' Sweden, to the Anglo-Americans.

Inside the Prinz Albrecht Strasse HQ there was only one man of power left who could do virtually what he wanted. That was if he was to betray the system which way would he go? He had no experience of the West, save those months in France as a young pilot back in the First World War. But he had plenty of contacts with the German communists, right up to the very top, including August Torgler, who had been accused of complicity in the Reichstag Fire of 1933, which had resulted in the banning of the KPD.†

So was Müller, who was in actual charge of the Gestapo in the inquiry into the Heydrich assassination, the one who ordered the swift murder of the survivors? Had he already been approached by the Russians, or did he make the approach himself? Several of his colleagues such as

---

* Menzies wanted to meet Canaris, but according to my informant, Fred Winterbotham of Ultra fame, Foreign Secretary Anthony Eden forbade the meeting.
† Torgler's son Kurt was brought to England by 'Red Ellen' Wilkinson, future Minister of Education in Attlee's 1945 cabinet. He returned to Germany indirectly and was killed in action on the Eastern Front as an NCO *in the German Army*! Yet another mystery.

Schellenberg, Hoettl and General Gehlen, the *Wehrmacht*'s Intelligence Supremo in the East, thought so.*

Did Heydrich's death mark a significant change in the career of Müller? The way to decide is to look at the remaining two and a half years of his career, as the most powerful policeman in the Reich after Himmler.

---

* The statements of these top Germans are to be treated with a certain amount of suspicion. Their post-war utterances were self-seeking, in the main, and were made in the climate of the Cold War.

THE MÜLLER FILE
TWO

Führer-Hauptquartier, den 9. November 1941

Ich befördere den

ᛋᛋ-Brigadeführer und Generalmajor der Polizei

Heinrich M ü l l e r
(ᛋᛋ-Nr. 1o7 o43)

zum

ᛋᛋ - G r u p p e n f ü h r e r

und

G e n e r a l l e u t n a n t der Polizei.

d.R.   gez.: Adolf Hitler

ᛋᛋ-Gruppenführer und
Generalleutnant der Waffen-ᛋᛋ

Appointment of Major-General Müller as Gruppenführer SS, signed
by Adolf Hitler

In July 1988, when Müller had supposedly been dead for over forty years, two British writers on the Nazi period received a phone call from the United States. They were Ian Sayer and Douglas Botting, who, together with the *Sunday Times* Insight Team, had done some interesting work on the missing Nazi millions at the end of the war. Their research as published in 1984 as a book under the title *Nazi Gold*. Perhaps it was the book which attracted the anonymous caller.

At that time they were researching the US Army's CIC (Counter Intelligence Corps), in particular this unit's work in post-war Germany. The Corps' task had been to apprehend Nazi suspects, try to recover Nazi loot and increasingly keep an eye on their erstwhile allies, the Russians, and the latter's efforts to use the beaten Germans for their own purposes. It goes without saying that secretly the Americans were doing the same. Around the nucleus of General Gehlen's Foreign Armies East organization, that strangely named Intelligence outfit on the German eastern front, Washington would build the future CIA.

As the two Britons wrote later in their book *America's Secret Army*, 'Even more controversial cases came to our attention in the course of our researches into this murky area. . . . This was the case of General Heinrich Müller, the overall chief of the Gestapo, who, as Adolf Eichmann's immediate superior, was responsible for the implementing of the "Final Solution" . . . and was thus by far the most

133

important war criminal still to be accounted for. Müller was last seen in Berlin shortly before the Russians captured the city and then vanished totally. Though nobody can be sure what happened to him after the end of the war, informed opinion has always favoured the view that he was spirited away to the USSR, where his special expertise in secret police work still had its uses.'

Thus the writers were 'somewhat surprised' when the anonymous phone call from the States reached them. The caller informed them that a 'large CIC file on Müller . . . had accidentally been released to him from the US archives'. One can imagine the writers' joy at this information. Researchers, especially forty years after the event, don't often get breaks of this magnitude.

For, according to the unknown American, 'the file consisted of 427 pages of documents.' They indicated that the Gestapo chief had survived the war and both he and another wanted war criminal, *Obergruppenführer* Odilo Globocnik, former SS and Police Leader in Lublin, head of Operation Reinhard, founder of the notorious extermination camps of Belzec, Solibor, Majdanek and Treblinka, and the man selected by Himmler to play a key role in the liquidation of the Polish Jews, had been retained by the CIC as intelligence advisers.

This was sensational stuff. Not only had the most important still-wanted Nazi war criminal been revealed as possibly still alive, but he and his Austrian subordinate had at one time worked for the American Corps, dedicated to the routing out of everything that the USA hated. It was, as the authors commented, as if someone had claimed that after the war Himmler had worked for Menzies' SIS.

Naturally the two rose to the fly, especially as the unknown informant 'continued by saying that he felt it was important that these documents should be published and that he had got in touch with acknowledged experts in the field of CIC history to discuss the possibility. He also informed us that US Army Intelligence and Security Command archives at Fort Meade, Maryland, did not appear to have a file in its possession.'

The unknown informant had not apparently attempted to contact the US media. He was seemingly more concerned with bringing the truth to the public's attention then making 'big bucks'. But Sayer and Botting were no fools. They knew the field and had done considerable research on post-war Germany, with Sayer in particular buying privately numbers of relevant documents not available to the general public.

So they told their caller 'that although we did have a CIC file on Müller, it amounted to no more than a few pages of inconsequential information.' As a result, they would be 'extremely interested' in receiving from him 'at least a summary of the contents of the documents he had acquired'.

But they were in for a disappointment. Their caller, who seems to have remained unnamed throughout the affair, was not as public-minded as he had appeared. He wanted not only to do his 'civic duty', but also wanted to make money doing so. Just before his documents from the supposed misdirected CIA file reached the two Britons in England, they learned that 'a leading British quality newspaper' (probably *The Times*) was working on the case. Also involved was one of America's top news magazines (*Time Magazine*).

The Times had been approached several months before and had seemingly offered £30,000 for research into the story. 'Subsequently,' the two authors went on, 'we were approached by a US government investigative agency, who sought our assistance in verifying certain aspects of the file, a copy of which they had recently acquired.'

On the face of it, therefore, the authors had fallen for yet another trap, one of the half-dozen or so dealing with the 'last secrets of the Reich' which had been hawked around Europe and the States, successfully and unsuccessfully, since the end of the Second World War.

Most have heard of the celebrated 'Hitler Diaries' con trick, which for a while fooled no less a person than the first investigator into the end of the Third Reich, Hugh Trevor-Roper, and Rupert Murdoch of *The Times*. He was quoted as snorting, 'I don't give a fuck if it's fake or not, so long as it sells papers!'

But who remembers the laughable case of the great US publishing house of Simon & Schuster, which bought the rights of a ludicrous book which claimed that its then

18-year-old author had been sent by Churchill in 1945 to smuggle *Reichsleiter* Martin Bormann out of Berlin. Thereafter Bormann was brought to Britain to 'help MI 6' and died peacefully a decade or so later to be buried in an outer London suburb. (Naturally the cemetery in which Hitler's 'Brown Eminence' is interred is still a secret.) Curiously enough, the same US publishing house had paid an equally large sum of money for the rights to Ladislas Farago's *The Fourth Reich* a quarter of a century earlier. In it the Hungarian-American writer described how he had actually *met* the missing Bormann in the South American jungle. As the *New York Times* announced in 1973, 'Bormann did not die in the ruins of Berlin. . . . He is alive today, living in Buenos Aires'. The London *Daily Telegraph* went one better. Its reviewer proclaimed: 'Farago tracked the fugitive Nazis across two continents, penetrating a remarkable world-wide conspiracy, and finally coming face to face with Bormann. . . . Fascinating!'

Fascinating indeed! One might well have asked the head of Simon & Schuster if he would please ask the real Bormann to stand up. But a decade or so ago there were enough gullible people around who still believed in conspiracy theories and governmental cover-ups.

But, as the top newspapers on both sides of the Atlantic appeared ready to fall for what seemingly was another fake set-up which would sell thousands of extra copies of their newspapers, the two British authors were sufficiently convinced by their unknown American contact to look carefully into the documents he had sent them.

They turned out to be very disappointing. 'An examination . . . revealed that it consisted of documents apparently signed by two genuine CIC agents in Region VIII (Berlin) towards the end of 1948 in connection with the employment of Müller and Globocnik as CIC advisers. One of these agents was Andrew Venters who was Dr Michael Arnaudow's case officer during the investigation into the whereabouts of Hitler's body; the other was Severin Wallach, who once ran a secret agent inside the office of the man who was to be the President of East Germany, Wilhelm Pieck.'

So far so good: two genuine agents involved back in the mid-forties in known CIC cases, which were still on file in Washington. The two authors must have felt that they were onto something big. According to their statement, one file sent to them and headed 'Soviet Investigations – Project UEBERSEE*, date 30 November 1948, read:

'Recent investigations by special teams of Soviet agents in the Western Zones† seeking definative(sic) information about the possible whereabouts of former SS Generals Heinrich MUELLER and Odlio (sic) Globocnik have apparently uncovered sufficient information to justify increased activity.

'Allegedly the Soviets have uncovered leads which cause them to suspect that the two above-named subjects were not killed at the end of the war. This is part of their ongoing probings in re(sic) the possible possession by the West of high-level Nazi leaders wanted by the Soviets either for trial or possible intelligence use by their agencies.'

So if we are to believe the two CIC agents, the Russians hadn't got hold of the missing man. Also, the file seems to prove that Müller survived the war. Understandably this startling information must have immediately brought to the minds of the two readers that overwhelming question: *how had Müller got away from Berlin and found succour in the camp of the enemy, namely the American CIC?*

But the file gave no answer. Indeed it avoided the whole issue. Instead, the unknown writer who had obtained this secret document skips the issue and lets his two quite low-ranking CIC agents make a lot of major policy-making suggestions: 'MUELLER's value to Western Intelligence is beyond doubt, but continued protection of GLOBOCNIK might prove to be an extreme embarrasment(sic). British intelligence . . . has become increasingly insistant(sic) that

---

* Overseas.
† Allied Zones of Occupation in Germany.

GLOBOCNIK either be terminated at once or relocated in such a manner as to totally remove him from the Soviet investigators area of research. . . .

'Original appraisals of former SS personnel with unsavory backgrounds such as GLOBOCNIK . . . should certainly be reconsidered, whereas the obvious value of MUELLER and SKORZENY* are self-evident and are clearly in line with policy recently set.'

The newspapers involved on both sides of the Atlantic were still sufficiently convinced by the file to invest more money in researching the story. The two authors, on the other hand, weren't. Their high hopes of making a major scoop had been dashed. As they wrote later: 'Though the agents' signatures and the typeface of the typewriter used to prepare the documents seemed authentic, the language was not typical, the spelling was bad and the "SECRET" security classification was not sufficiently high and not printed in the normal typeface.'

The language was definitely in advance of the time, 1948. The age of bland euphemism had not yet arrived. The use of the word 'terminated' was premature. 'Downsizing,' 'visually impaired,' 'collatoral casualties' and other 'junk' words of our own time were still to come.

There were two other major areas which made Botting and Sayer feel they couldn't really trust the information. The documents were all photocopies and were no use to the forensic experts. The two CIC agents were indeed genuine, but they had been carefully picked. They were both long dead.

It was the old ploy: a sensation, allied to real people, within a framework of events that had really taken place. Unfortunately the real people were all dead and unable to confirm or deny the sensation. Thereafter, those who were taken in would have to shell out large sums of money to the purveyor of the sensation in order to obtain the evidence which would confirm it. Naturally, it could never be confirmed. As Goebbels had long maintained in his years as Minister of Propaganda and Public Enlightenment, 'If you are going to tell a lie, tell a big one.'

* Otto Skorzeny, the head of the SS's own SAS, the 'Hunting Commando'.

138

The two authors concluded, 'It was our considered judgement that, on various grounds, the Alleged CIC Müller file was a forgery. Our view was corroborated by Colonel Earl Browning, who was Operations Chief at CIC Headquarters in Frankfurt at the time the documents were supposed to have been produced. Colonel Browning made it clear to us that, as head of CIC operations, all special activities in Germany would have come to his attention – certainly something as sensitive as the employment of Heinrich Müller and Odilo Globocnik as CIC advisers.'

Yet the story is of some significance in the hunt for Müller. For whoever that unknown confidence trickster was, he had known quite a lot about his subject. He had, indeed, known enough about it to doubt the two standard features of the Müller Case: (1) that the missing man had headed eastwards to the Russians in 1945 as had been suggested and (2) that Müller would never have headed westward to approach the Western Allies because his crimes against the Jews in general and, as we shall see, against British PoWs in particular, were so horrific that he would have been arrested immediately.

The alleged CIC file raises yet another matter that up to that time had never been considered – where had Müller been concealed, presumably somewhere in Western Europe, between 1945 and 1948?

1941: THE RED ORCHESTRA STARTS TO PERFORM.

'We've got the pianists, *Reichsführer*, but where's the conductor?'

Müller to Himmler, 1942.

ONE

It was nearly midnight. Everything was in place. In the immediate area of Number 101 Rue de Atrebates in Brussels a company of German HQ troops were in position. They were armed, excited and all of them had socks pulled over their jackboots.

Hauptmann der Reserve Harry Piepe, in charge of the raid, thought they looked funny in the socks, but he kept his opinion to himself. After all they were 'rear echelon stallions'. This would be the only kind of action they'd probably see in this war; let them have their fun.

The year before he had been busy rounding up survivors and stragglers at Dunkirk after they had chased the Tommies back to their island. But in the meantime they had told him he was too old for active service. So they'd transferred him to a unit of which he had never even heard – something called the *Abwehr*. Now he was in that strange organization's counter-espionage department, engaged in his first clandestine operation in this quiet Brussels backstreet. Around him the Belgian capital slept. Naturally there was a curfew for both civilians and soldiers. The only people still around would be people like himself, involved in undercover ops, or military policemen checking the brothels and the like for deserters. For, with the new war in Russia escalating, the average German Infantryman would do anything, even risk a spell in the hated Torgau Military Prison, not to be sent to the Eastern Front.

143

Piepe's plan was simple. For nearly two weeks the Luftwaffe's detection vans had been patrolling the area until they had finally located the 'pianist', as the *Abwehr* called a clandestine radio operator, in the narrow three-storey house. In due course he and his men would rush it, hoping to catch the occupants in their beds. They had thought of everything. They'd even brought roof-axes with them in case anyone attempted to escape through the attic on to the roof and from there to the house next door. He knew from his older and more experienced comrades in the *Abwehr* that this was an old trick. Anyway, Piepe reassured himself, nothing would go wrong. He'd succeed through speed and simple brute force.

Time passed slowly. Piepe found himself glancing repeatedly at the glowing dial of his wrist watch. There was no sound save the breathing of the Secret Field Police hidden in the nearest doorways. Then it was zero hour.

In an instant all was noise and confusion. An *Abwehr* officer at the door of No 101 called, 'In here, in here!' They rushed in. A 'half-naked beautiful woman' lay on a camp bed on the ground floor. She was 'Jewish, typically Jewish'. She was handcuffed even before she was really awake. They blundered up the stairs, jostling each other in their haste.

A transmitter! Piepe's sergeant put his hand on it. It was still warm. There were papers scattered on the floor. All were in German! There was even an instruction leaflet for a radio operator, also in German.

They clattered up the stairs to the second floor. Another woman, about 28. She, too, looked very Jewish. As Piepe said later, 'She was a German emigrant'. He meant a Jewess who had fled from Germany.

'We've got him!' Piepe forgot the woman and followed the others. A man stood there defiantly, handcuffed. He was bleeding about the face. According to the sergeant, he had put up a fight. Piepe thought it better not to ask too many questions. He returned to the woman on the floor below. She was sobbing now, declaring, 'I'm glad it's over. I never wanted to be a member of the ring, but my boyfriend made me join.'

144

At six they left with their prisoners, leaving three men to wait in the house in case anyone turned up. At HQ a delighted *Hauptmann der Reserve* Piepe reported to his chief.

The latter was also puzzled by all the documents in German and the fact that both women were native Germans, but he was pleased by Piepe's success. Almost immediately after the latter had reported, he began to draft a cable in code to Admiral Canaris in Berlin. While he was doing so, a caller turned up at Number 101. He looked and stank like a tramp. Over his shoulder he had a wicker basket full of rabbits. He asked if the lady was in. She wasn't, the police told him. He tried to argue. In the end, the cops lost their temper and kicked him on his way. He was the organization's lookout man.

But what was that organization?

Back at HQ, with the message to Berlin on its way, the two *Abwehr* men discussed the case. They knew the 'pianist' and his two Jewish assistants couldn't be working for the British, or they wouldn't have been caught so easily. Everyone knew the 'English Secret Service' was the best in the world; even the Führer acknowledged that. They had to be Russians. So they pondered what they would call this newly discovered clandestine outfit.

In *Abwehr* jargon a spy ring which used a transmitter was called an 'orchestra' because it used the radio operators known as 'pianists'. Piepe's superior suggested the 'Russian Orchestra'. Piepe disagreed. Instead he proposed 'Red Orchestra', which his boss accepted. Thus the ring was christened. The two German counter-intelligence agents had given name to an organization that operated not only in Belgium, but throughout Europe, indeed, as we shall see, throughout the whole of the western world, and whose final operative was arrested in a remote English village only in 1999, aged nearly ninety!

But as the two officers named the Soviet espionage ring that had been in place as far back as 1937/38 a fourth caller presented himself at Number 101 Rue de Atrebates. He bullied his way into the house, producing papers identifying him as a member of the German Todt Organization.* The embarrassed cop arrested him, but not for long. He demanded that the policeman call his superior at the *Abwehr* HQ, which he did and was told to let the self-important civilian go. Of course, he was a member of the 'Red Orchestra', who had seen all he needed and off he went.

The report on the arrests in Brussels, plus the fact that the operatives were German and there were important documents in that language at Number 101, caused a sensation in Berlin. Immediately this startling discovery was classified as *'Geheime Reichssache'* (roughly 'top secret'). Hitler himself was informed. He ordered: 'This cancer must be destroyed at once!'

But it wasn't as easy as that. The 'Red Orchestra' affair would go on for months, even years. Perhaps, as we shall see, it never really ended. In the meanwhile, however, Piepe had returned to 101 Rue de Atrebates and made further discoveries, in particular a piece of charred paper on which he could just make out a series of number groupings. He realized at once that these belonged to some sort of a code and forwarded the paper to the *Abwehr*'s decoding office. The result, after six weeks, would provide the *Abwehr* and Müller's Gestapo, which had now become involved on Hitler's orders, with yet another shock.

The code experts in Berlin were able to decipher a third of the 'Red Orchestra's' messages. These related directly to massive Soviet espionage in Berlin itself.

Now the matter was taken up at the very highest level at Prinz Albrecht Strasse. As Schellenberg wrote after the war: 'After Heydrich's assassination in May 1942, Himmler had taken on the job of co-ordinating and supervising the *Rote Kapelle* [Red Orchestra]. Very soon tension arose between him and Müller, which worsened to such an extent that sometimes when Müller and I were reporting to him together, Müller, many years my senior, would be sent out of the room

---

* Named after Doctor Todt who had built the Westwall and would soon plan the Atlantic Wall, intended to stop Allied landings on the coast of 'Fortress Europe'.

so that Himmler could discuss matters with me alone. Müller was intelligent enough to recognize this situation and whenever he had anything particularly difficult to bring up would ask me to do it for him. Once, with an ironical smile, he said to me, "Obviously he likes your face better than my Bavarian mug".'

For a man who allegedly loved to take the credit for other people's achievements, Müller kept strangely in the background in this, the major spy investigation of the whole war. In July 1942, for instance, Himmler ordered Müller and Schellenberg to fly to Hitler's HQ in East Prussia to give the Führer a comprehensive report on the 'Red Orchestra' situation.

As Schellenberg recorded, 'We had only a few hours to get the report ready and, when we met, Müller began by telling me how invaluable my reports on the *Rote Kapelle* had always been to him and how very comprehensive my knowledge of Russian spying methods seemed to be. After a few more obvious flatteries he asked me to take the report to Himmler for both of us. But I said that as I was responsible for only about thirty percent of what had been achieved, he might as well report on the matter himself.'

'No,' he said, 'you'll get the red carpet. I'll probably get the boot.'

At the time Schellenberg, knowing that it was unusual for Müller to hide his light under a bushel, was puzzled by Müller's reluctance. But he did suspect that Müller seemed to be wanting to pull out of this key investigation of the Russian Secret Service. It was the first mention among those in the know that Müller might not be all he seemed to be, that he, too, now that Heydrich was dead, might have come to some arrangement with the Russians known to be in Prague.

Himmler seemed to feel that nothing was wrong. Indeed it appeared to Schellenberg, who was now busy cultivating the *Reichsführer* SS, that the latter felt he was still dealing with the same old selfish careerist. With a sneer, he asked Schellenberg, 'Are you responsible for this report or is Müller?'

Schellenberg replied that he was.

'That is typical of him,' Himmler snapped. 'To belittle other people's achievements so as to put himself in the most favourable light. A thoroughly petty attitude and you can tell him I said so.'

It must have been music to Schellenberg's ears, for secretly he hated Müller and wished him out of the way so he could be top dog in the Prinz Albrecht Strasse. He didn't tell him Himmler's words, of course. Müller possessed even more power now that Heydrich was dead and it didn't do to run foul of him and the officers under his control.

But the interview on the report to be presented to the Führer, as related by Schellenberg, does reveal two things. One, that Müller and the Gestapo were falsifying their reports on the Red Orchestra, especially about the discovery of that spy organization's Berlin branch. And two, that although Müller was behind the falsifying, he didn't want to be too closely associated, for the record at least, with the discovery of the Berlin branch. Now in this middle and decisive year of the war, when victory or defeat for Nazi Germany lay on a knife's edge, Müller was clearly making a personal decision. He had long known – after all he had been a professional for over twenty years now – that knowledge bought absolution, even freedom, for criminals. Turning state's evidence against fellow criminals had often ensured leniency for the most hardened crook. If Germany were defeated and he was forced to try and save his own neck, the question now arose – to whom should he turn? To the Western Allies or to those who he had persecuted all his working life, the Reds?

148

TWO

The Gestapo and its boss knew them scornfully as *'Salonkommunisten'*. But if the members of Berlin's 'Red Orchestra' were indeed 'parlour pinks', they were immensely powerful and the keys to many sources of vital information for a beleaguered Moscow, now that Soviet Russia was fighting for its life against the Nazi invaders.

The German spies, mostly middle-class and non-Jewish, were led by Harro Schulze-Boysen, an officer in Goering's Air Ministry, Arvid Harnack, a high-ranking beaurocrat in the Ministry of Economic Warfare, and Adam Kuckhoff, writer and director of *Pragfilm*, a movie company which came under the orders of arch womanizer Dr Goebbels, Minister of Propaganda and Public Enlightment.

On the surface the positions of these three were not at the highest level, but each had access to top-level information which was vital to the Kremlin at that stage. Schulze-Boysen knew about the Germans' spy flights and parachute drops behind the Russian lines; Harnack was intimately acquainted with the illegal shipments of gold and currency transactions in so-called neutral countries, which Germany needed to keep her war industry running, while Kuckhoff was well placed to know about German movie stars' private lives, leaving them open to Russian blackmail.

Outwardly, therefore, they seemed to the casual observer to be the usual crowd of rich party-goers one would find in any capital city. Harnack's Jewish-American wife, for instance, was later made out to be a very active lesbian by the Gestapo. But in 1942/43 they were passing on their brittle anti-Nazi chatter and gossip, plus a great deal of hard information, to a nation which was bleeding the *Wehrmacht* white on the *Ostfront*.

By this time, after the Brussels discoveries that had shocked the Führer, two of the Gestapo's key men, Panziger and Koppkow, were working on the Berlin Red Orchestra. They were both seasoned experts in the German anti-communist campaign and had been instrumental in liquidating the German KPD after 1933. They worked directly under the Gestapo's acknowledged leader in this field, Müller himself.

As was to be expected, the members of the Berlin Red Orchestra turned out to be easier to detect than the average communist cell in, say, working-class Hamburg.* The *salon-pinks* had no internal security and didn't see the need for small individual and virtually independent cells. They even spent drunken nights posting up anti-Hitler posters and slogans in Central Berlin, almost as if they *wanted* to be caught. And they talked, regardless of the fact that Müller had by now infiltrated informers into their ranks.

By this time the Gestapo had acquired most of the facts they needed, but they knew that they must have hard-and-fast evidence to arrest Schulze-Boysen, the grand nephew of Admiral von Tirpitz, the founder of the modern German Navy, and Harnack, the nephew of one of the country's most distinguished theologians. At the same time they had pinpointed the other members of the organization, some of whom actually worked in German Intelligence and perhaps had access to the Gestapo's own secrets. But still Müller was hesitant to act decisively and wipe out the whole Red

---

* The author's uncle, an old-time communist, ran such a cell in the small upper-class town of Reinbek, just outside Hamburg. He was captured by the Gestapo and was sent off to a concentration camp (he survived). But his cell, feeding working-class Hamburg with anti-Nazi propaganda from the little dormitory town, continued well into 1944 before it was betrayed by an informer. It appears there were many such cells in Germany.

Orchestra, which had branches in virtually every German-occupied country. For the Russians had perfected a ploy which the British had pioneered in the First World War. This was to run active spies in an enemy country from a neutral one. Here, if the spies were caught, they could expect a much milder sentence than the death penalty probably meted out in the enemy's homeland. Thus, while Belgium and Holland were no longer neutral, but occupied by 1942, the transmitters which had been located there prior to the German occupation were used to transmit information gained in Berlin to Moscow and to pass on orders from the same source.

Now Müller was ready to wind up the Berlin traitors' activities. The Führer, who had no sense of intelligence operations, was breathing down his neck,[*] while Müller was wondering whether he could gain any other advantage from the anti-Red Orchestra operation.

Of course he knew of the major sting being currently run by the *Abwehr* in Holland, 'Operation North Pole'.[†] Here some fifty 'turned' Dutch agents working for the British were being used to transmit false information back to London. Was there a chance he might do the same with captured Russian 'pianists'?

In the end Müller decided that he would play a so-called 'radio game' with Moscow. He closed down all anti-Red Orchestra operations in Belgium and Holland (perhaps not to compromise 'Operation North Pole', for the British were already on to the Red Orchestra and Müller feared that any indiscretion in the Low Countries might endanger the *Abwehr*'s own major radio game[‡]).

---

[*] Hitler always refused to shake hands even with own senior intelligence agents, save Skorzeny, the man who rescued Mussolini.

[†] See the author's *Hitler's Dirty War* (Pen & Sword) for further details.

[‡] In print at least no one has yet tackled the massive scale of *all* Red Orchestra ops. Not only do they include the Continentals, but they involve Philby, Maclean, Burgess and Blunt in the UK, but also Alger Hiss, Harry Dexter White and even an ex-officer of the OSS, next to the chief 'Wild Bill' Donovan, in the States. In retrospect, it seems that the Russians not only

On 19 November 1942 when the Red Army began its major attack on the German Sixth Army under General Paulus at Stalingrad, which would lead to the fall of that city and the start of Germany's military defeat, the doorbell rang at the office of Simex Export-Import at Number 78 Avenue, Champs Elysées.

It was the Gestapo, twelve of them, and their French 'poodles' from the Parisian police. 'We're the police,' the blond man in charge announced.

Madame Mignon who opened the door to them, retained her *sangfroid*. She replied, 'No need to tell me that. Do you think I can't smell?'

The crackdown on the Red Orchestra had begun.

This time the Gestapo acted as the conquered European always feared they would. One of the first suspects arrested recorded what happened to him at the hands of *Kommissar* Jung and his French henchmen (the undermanned Gestapo, with 1,000 agents for the whole of France, made good use of French cops and turncoats).

The suspect was asked where one of the major members of the organization was. He said he didn't know. 'Jung opened a drawer, took out a length of rope and secured my legs with it. Then he grabbed a stick and made as if to wedge it between the bonds. This is known as the "tourniquet" torture: the interrogator turns the stick until the rope tightens to breaking and bites deep into the victim's flesh. Before setting to work, however, the German turned on the radio to full blast. An English voice began to thunder. The set was tuned to the BBC.'

And so it went on. Keller, the suspect, wasn't the only one. All over Paris men and women were arrested. Even children were taken into custody if they were thought to be of use in blackmailing their parents into talking. And of course they did

---

had spies everywhere in the West, but agents of influence who might well have become heads of both post-war Anglo-American intelligence services and senior cabinet holders in the post-war US government, if they hadn't been found out by the *Venona* de-codes, which are still partially classified in the USA, home of the 'Freedom of Information Act'.

talk. While the condemned of the Berlin Red Orchestra were executed by the State Executioner the Parisian Red Orchestra captives mostly agreed to cooperate with the Gestapo and help with Müller's radio game.*

So the Russian 'pianists' in Brussels and Amsterdam were turned and as a reward were treated gently by their Gestapo captors. One of the captors recorded after the war, 'The prisoners' love for their work became a real passion. They were treated reasonably well, they had a certain amount of freedom and their relations with the German officers supervising them improved as time went on.' Once or twice prisoners attempted to escape and some actually did. But, just as was the case with the Germans forced into the British 'Double Cross Committee's' radio game in the UK, the enemy 'pianists' seemed content to do exactly as they were told. Perhaps they thought that, if they survived until the end of the war, they'd be safe. If their own side won, all would be well and good. If the Germans were the victors, they'd reward those who had helped them in this strange radio game with Moscow with their freedom or a light prison sentence instead of death, perhaps even with total freedom.

The Gestapo radio game would continue until the liberation of Paris in August 1944. From 1941 until about early 1943 Müller was in charge. He was responsible for the day-to-day technical side of the operation. Meanwhile, the political responsibility was changing hands. As Müller's boss, Himmler, had been in charge from the start, but his main concern was the political side.

By the time it became apparent that Germany was beginning to lose the war Himmler started to use the radio deception for a secret political purpose: to reach a

* Some of the German women captives, according to post-war rumours, got their guards to make love to them in the hope that they would become pregnant. If they did, they knew German law wouldn't allow them to be executed till after the birth. One senior female prisoner was enamoured of her young SS guard. The Gestapo turned a blind eye and it was reputed that he made love to her in the sealed 'Green Minna' (Black Maria) taking her to meet the executioner and his axe.

153

compromise peace with the West. In order to do this he needed information to feed material into this *Funkspiel*, as the Germans called it. This material, mainly political, had to come from the various Berlin ministries, in particular von Ribbentrop's Foreign Ministry.

But there was a catch. By this time Hitler, hidden away at his various headquarters, was too busy conducting the shooting war to bother about intelligence games. He left the day-to-day business of running the Reich and its ministries to Bormann.

Thus it was, with certain exceptions, Bormann started to take over the direction of what material should be fed to the 'pianists'. Even his secretaries knew nothing of what was going on. The only people in the know, apart from Müller and his underlings, were von Ribbentrop and a small group of experts. Their files were kept locked in a safe, labelled top secret and code-named 'Operation Bear'.

Slowly but surely, Müller began to gravitate to Bormann, not only as the source of information for the great radio game, but also as the coming man in Nazi politics. Goering and Himmler might think they still had a role to play, and, of course, they had. But the man of the future was Martin Bormann, who, like Müller, kept himself well in the background. His name rarely appeared in the press. When photos did appear, Bormann and Müller were well in the background and hardly ever identified. Edward Crankshaw, the first British historian of the Gestapo, once wrote of Müller a sentence that could well be applied to Bormann: 'He left hardly any trace behind him. Nothing is known of him – neither where he came from . . . where he disappeared.'

This is not quite accurate,* but it is basically true of both men, born in the same year to similar provincial families. Such men were created to understand each other.

But on the surface they didn't seem to. Müller often maintained that 'Bormann knows his own mind, but he hasn't got

---

* See C. Whiting: *The Hunt for Martin Bormann* (Pen & Sword) for further details.

154

what it takes.' Yet, within six months after the spring of 1943, when Müller said this to Schellenberg one evening in Berlin, he was working hand-in-glove with Bormann to prevent what seemed a German attempt to make an approach for peace to the West in Switzerland.

On a spring night just after the German defeat at Stalingrad, it appears, if we are to believe Schellenberg, that Müller let his hair down in an almost treasonable fashion. They were discussing the Berlin branch of the Red Orchestra. Müller observed that many of its members were middle-class and intellectually inclined. He remarked that 'The Soviet influence in Western Europe has spread to the educated classes.' It was a truism, but unlike Müller to discuss such matters.

Indeed he went on to speculate that 'communism presents a kind of positive electric current to the negative current of the West. You're an educated man, you've studied law and you've travelled. Look at the members of the Red Orchestra whom you knew. They were intellectuals, too, but of a different kind, progressives seeking a definite solution, and they died still believing it possible.'

Schellenberg must have been shocked, but he kept silent and let Müller ramble on. 'I must say that I see Stalin in a different light now. He's greatly superior to all the leaders of the Western nations and, if you want my opinion, I think we should come to terms with him. You always know where you are with the Russians, at least. They either cut off your head or embrace you.'

Schellenberg felt 'increasingly nervous' at Müller's 'sudden change of attitude'. 'What is he getting at?' he asked himself, as Müller 'kept emptying his glass. He had never been so talkative before.'

Schellenberg tried to lighten the situation, and said, 'That's fine. Let's all shout "*Heil Stalin!*" and Boss Müller will become cock of the walk at the KKVD.'*

Müller looked at him. He 'had a nasty glint in his eye.'

---

* Russian secret police, forerunner of the KGB.

'That'd be fine,' he retorted, 'and you'd be for the high jump, you and your blasted bourgeois friends.'

As Schellenberg said of the end of that meeting, 'I came away from that odd discussion still not knowing just what Müller had been getting at, but I understood some months later.'

THREE

In essence Müller regarded himself as first and foremost a policeman. By 1944 he had been a policeman for a quarter of a century, but he was also a leading member of the 'General SS'.* Not only did he seek out enemies of the state, he also had to put his signature to those infamous decrees that condemned thousands, even hundreds of thousands, to a living death behind the barbed wire of the concentration camps. He was Himmler's subordinate and Eichmann's superior and was as much responsible for the Final Solution as they were; hence his post-war classification as 'senior war criminal'.

Looking through the files of the Simon Wiesenthal Center, one can clearly see his signature and rank attached to ageing documents directing the arrest of Belgian and Dutch Jews, the deportation of German Jews and so on, and he was one of the leading participants of the infamous Wannsee Conference of January 1942, where the last details of the Final Solution were worked out under Heydrich's leadership.

So Müller bears as much responsibility for what went on in the death camps as Eichmann. Yet, as far as the author has been able to ascertain, he never made a public statement expressing his hatred of the Jews or any other of the 'third class' citizens from the east, who were worked to death in the war factories of German industry or disappeared in the

* *Allgemeine SS*, to distinguish it from the fighting SS, the *Waffen SS*.

concentration camps. This might be explained by his notorious secrecy and the rules of normal police procedure which ensure that policemen do not make public statements.

Whether Müller was anti-semitic is not known. We *do* know, however, that by the spring of 1944 he was being forced into actions that would ensure that the Allies would classify him as a war criminal, and this time the crimes were directed not against helpless civilians but young Allied servicemen.

On 4 March 1944 Müller issued a written order which later became known as the *'Kugelerlass'* (the Bullet Decree). It was an instruction to the Security Police, SD and Gestapo that certain categories of Allied prisoners of war were to 'be discharged from prisoner-of-war status' and handed over to the control of the Gestapo. Thereafter the *Wehrmacht* would have no control over their future. It must be noted at this juncture that there were immediate protests from a couple of elderly German generals concerned mainly with Western Allied prisoners.

In the main the order was directed at Soviet PoWs, who were notoriously badly treated. But Polish PoWs engaged in sabotage of German war plants were also included. The 'Bullet Decree', however, could also be applied, together with Hitler's secret 'Commando Order' of two years previously, to British and American Pows. They could also be 'discharged from prisoner-of-war status' and 'handed over to the Gestapo'. And to make sure that officers in the *Wehrmacht*, including PoW camp commandants, complied with the new measures, it was stated: 'In the case of non-compliance with this order, I shall bring to trial before a court martial any commander or other officer who has either failed to carry out his duty in instructing the troops about this order or who had acted contrary to it.'

As a sop to the conscience of those involved, and naturally to protect them as well if they ever fell into Allied hands, instructions were issued that the cause of death of any PoW in these circumstances should always be recorded with that old formula, 'shot while trying to escape'. In the case of paratroopers and Allied commandos taken while on a mission behind German lines, their deaths would be entered in official records as 'killed in action'. The scene was set for what was later to become known as 'the Great Escape'.

A survivor, now 82, Frank Day, recalled the moment when the 'Great Escape' began to go 'pear-shaped.' He was lying on a trolley, 30 foot underground, halfway along the narrow escape tunnel that led out of Stalag Luft III. Already 76 fellow Allied officers had left the camp. The young Squadron Leader was scheduled to be the next to go.

Frank Day possessed no elaborate disguise or papers. He didn't even speak German. Wearing an Army greatcoat, he was simply planning to walk 30 miles to the nearest *Luftwaffe* field and steal an enemy plane. As he recalled over half a century later, 'I was capable of flying anything, provided that there was enough fuel. But what would have happened if I had turned up in England flying a German plane I just don't know.'

But the young officer, who had been shot down over Crete in 1942 and wounded in the leg, wasn't worried about that eventuality that March night. He was concentrating on escape, knowing that he was lucky to have been selected for the tunnel because, when he arrived at Stalag Luft III, the escape committee had taken one look at his leg and announced, 'You can't escape with your leg like that.'

Day, however, had worked hard to convince them that he was fit enough to do a bunk. He'd worked hard as a 'penguin', one of those who walked around in a penguin-like manner distributing earth from the tunnel from bags concealed beneath their trouser-legs. He had helped with disguises and survived on what amounted to starvation rations in the intervals between Red Cross parcels. So he was called to join the escape party.

Now he waited at the mid-point in the tunnel, predictably called 'Piccadilly Circus'. He moved on to begin to exit and 'had just got onto the trolley when I heard a lot of commotion and shooting. . . . I thought, Fuck it, I'm not going out there!' So he pulled back, 'and as I came out there were a lot of goons shouting "*Raus*" and so on.'

The Great Escape, as it would become known to every new

generation of British TV viewers, thanks to Steve McQueen on his motorbike in the customary Christmas Day movie of that name, had begun. Fortunately for Day, 'I was sent to the cooler for two days' solitary confinement.' He was in luck.

Many of those who did get out were not. They were shot in cold blood. 'We were sent a copy of the *Frankfurter Zeitung* with a list of those who had been killed. We were absolutely horrified. It was supposed to be your duty to try to escape. Everyone thought, "Bloody hell!"'

Bloody hell indeed for those who fell into the hands of the Gestapo, especially if they were re-taken in remote places where there weren't too many witnesses and the police officials could do what they wanted, particularly as they were under orders to carry out the death sentence or pay the consequence themselves.

Fifty of the men who escaped (only three succeeded in making a home run from Stalag Luft III at Sagan in Poland) were shot. All were said to have been killed while trying to run away. In fact they were first picked up, handed over to the Gestapo and then shot, usually in the back of the head. They were then cremated and their ashes returned to the PoW camp to deter the others.

One of the escapees got as far as German-speaking Alsace, which had formerly been part of France. Here he was captured and taken to the Gestapo HQ in Strasbourg. Berlin, ie Müller, told the local head of the Gestapo what to do with the recaptured officer. 'The British prisoner-of-war who has been handed over to the Gestapo by the Strasbourg Criminal Police, by superior orders, is to be taken immediately in the direction of Breslau and to be shot *en route* while escaping. An undertaker is directed to remove the body to a crematorium and have it cremated there, The urn is to be sent to the head of the Criminal Police Headquarters RSHA. The contents of this teleprint and the affair itself are to be made known only to the officials directly concerned with the carrying out of this matter, and they are to be pledged to secrecy by special handshake.'

In due course the prisoner was executed on his way to the ovens at Natzweiler Concentration Camp, the only one on

French soil. He was allowed out of the car to relieve himself and, while one member of the Gestapo chatted to him, another shot him from behind.*

Four months later, also in Alsace, thirty-five members of the 1st SAS Regiment suffered the same fate. Indeed the casualties incurred at the hands of the German firing squad amounted to sixty-four percent of the troopers dropped to help the local Resistance and the advance of the US 7th Army, coming up from the south, heading for the German frontier. This time the murders of the British PoWs were carried out by the *Wehrmacht*, members of the German 80th Corps under the command of a General Gallenkamp.

But Gallenkamp and the officers who directed the shootings were acting directly under orders from Berlin and were too concerned with the safety of their own hides (unlike some German officers who took a great risk and disobeyed the 'Bullet Decree' and 'Commando Order No.30') to refuse to carry out the dreadful deed. Thus on 7 July 1944 the Germans summoned SAS officer 20-year-old Lieutenant Crisp, still limping from a leg wound inflicted during the skirmish in which he and the rest of the young SAS troopers had been taken, and told him that he and his comrades were going to be shot.

Crisp returned to his comrades and told them what was going to happen. They shook hands, smoked a last cigarette and then lined up, thirty British and one US fighter pilot, also a prisoner. There had been some debate among the Germans whether he should be executed, but in the end they decided he should. Perhaps they wanted no witnesses to their crime. To their front a German officer called the firing squad to order. '*Leg an,*' he commanded and his men took aim.

Later one of the German witnesses reported to General Gallenkamp, who had conveniently absented himself from the area that dawn, 'The parachutists died in an exemplary, brave and calm manner.' The same witness told Gallenkamp

---

* It can be assumed that some of the policemen involved had been born French and that the escaper had come to the Continent to help 'liberate' them, his own killers. It was, in part, Frenchmen, too, who delivered British SOE agents, men *and* women, to Natzweiler to be executed.

that 'their bearing had been impeccable' and added, 'General, you may be assured that this was the most terrible day and hardest hour of my life.'

A week later three of the wounded SAS men, who couldn't walk out to be shot, Troopers Ogg, Pascoe and Williams, and who, unattended, were tormented by maggots under their blood-stained bandages, were put into 'a twilight sleep', as the German report put it. That 'twilight sleep to ease pain' turned out to be a lethal injection. They were murdered as they lay there. Later that July their bodies were disposed of secretly. No records were kept of how or where.

But by that July, when already the first of the SAS investigators and future hunters of the German killers were beginning to interest themselves in the fate of their thirty-five comrades, Müller had begun to realize that he was in trouble with the English.

He and Nebe, of the *Kripo*, had been the ones who had chosen the recaptured men of the 'Great Escape' to be shot. An eyewitness, Peter Mohr of the *Kripo*, on whose evidence the later court case against the Gestapo would be based, recalled how Nebe had looked at the 'mugshots' and personal details of the PoWs, selecting the ones to be executed 'while escaping' with 'He's too young. Not to be shot,' 'He looks Jewish, shoot him,' 'He's got kids, return him to camp,' and so on.

But Mohr also remembered how Müller had called him to his home in Berlin where the Gestapo chief lived with his mistress and their two young children. Müller had told him that the British were now making a great fuss about the dead PoWs. Churchill had mentioned the matter in the House of Commons. The British had also contacted the International Red Cross and von Ribbentrop, the Nazi Foreign Minister, was so embarrassed that he demanded an explanation from an equally worried Himmler.

Müller was now forced to act. Mohr was present in his office in the Prinz Albrecht Strasse when he ordered that new reports on the 'Sagan shootings' had to be prepared immediately. 'You and your officials must be in a position to reconstruct the process of the shootings. An international commission is expected to arrive. The new reports will no

162

longer be treated as secret, but as ordinary teleprinter messages – and the shootings will also no longer be kept secret, as this would appear suspicious to a commission.'

As Mohr's statement to the British authorities explained, Müller then gave detailed instructions as to how the answers to the Swiss Protecting Power should be prepared and drafted. Firstly the new documents must show the 'basic necessity for the killings'. Secondly details must be given, as, for example, the story of one officer being drowned while trying to swim a river and another killed in a motor accident.

In other words, Müller was preparing a second *open* file on the men who had escaped and been recaptured. This second open file even contained the names of the Gestapo officers who had taken part in the arrests and shootings. They were full of expressions of regret and of the soul-searching that had afflicted these unfortunates after they had been 'forced' by attacks on their persons by these desperate PoWs to use their weapons or had been unable to stop them when they had plunged to their deaths on railway lines or into rivers in their haste to escape.

It was a clever ploy to prepare this second thick file of 'precise' details with the comprehensive statements of the Gestapo officers concerned, while keeping the first and true one, which had been presented to an angry Führer, secret. But it was not going to work. For on the other side of the Channel a benign old Scot, bespectacled and gentle, who looked as if he should be wearing slippers instead of the field service dress of a full colonel, didn't believe one word of the second file. For two years he had been following up the alleged murders of British commandos, paras, SAS men and the like who had fallen into German hands and had been reported 'killed while attempting to escape'. He had encountered too many such cases. Now these fifty dead Allied PoWs were the last straw.

In a mansion in Kensington Palace Gardens (not far from the present German Embassy) the old Colonel added new details to his already voluminous file on the subject.

Müller had met his match at last. Now he, the long-time hunter, was being hunted.

THE MÜLLER FILE
THREE

In the last days of September 1963 an unusual event took place in the *Garnisonfriedhof* in Berlin-Neukoelln. Indeed, none of the cemetery attendants who had worked there since the war could remember one like it. Without any notice a typical, marble-stoned grave, number one in the sixth row, had been sealed off by Berlin policemen. Carefully the stone was placed to one side and the legend it bore covered with a cloth. Then the four rose plants which had adorned the grave since 1958 and which had been tended lovingly by a middle-aged Berlin woman once a month ever since, were also dug up. They, too, were carefully placed out of the way of the police who were waiting to take over.

It was a macabre scene, typical of one of the old Hollywood horror movies: the open grave concealed behind a sacking wall, the stern-looking cops, the police photographer waiting for orders and the little crowd of subdued official witnesses and onlookers.

There were no tears on the faces of the crowd, just stony resignation, and on that of the pretty middle-aged woman, the only one save for the official stenographer from the Berlin Ministry of Justice, a kind of faint apprehension. There should have been another woman present, one who knew more than anyone about the dead man who had lain there since 1945 and the one who had erected that black marble tombstone with its gold lettering five years before. But she had not been invited to the ceremony. Indeed, she might well be taken into custody soon for discreet interrogation, not only by the German authorities but by those of what the Germans called 'a service friendly to us'.

The woman who was present was, in a way, the star of the show and undoubtedly some of those present, who knew of her role back in the last years of the Second World War, must have cast furtive glances in her direction and asked themselves why exactly was she there.

Once, in Hitler's time, she had been a minor movie star in those flippant love stories which Goebbels had produced to take the nation's mind off the grim realities of the total war which he himself had called for.* But she had been more than that. She had also been 'B' or 'MB', the youthful mistress of the second most powerful man in the Third Reich, Martin Bormann.

In a letter written to his wife Gerda in faraway Obersalzberg, where she tended their six kids and often went barefoot in the peasant fashion in the summer meadows, Bormann described how he had taken 'M'. 'I kissed her without further ado and quite scorched her with my burning joy. I fell madly in love with her. I arranged it so I met her again many times and then I took her in spite of her refusals. You know the strength of my will against which M was of course powerless. . . . Now she is mine and now – lucky fellow – now I am, or rather I feel, doubly and unbelievably happily married. . . . What do you think, beloved, of your crazy fellow?'

Gerda Bormann apparently felt it was all right. She replied, 'I am so fond of M myself that I cannot be angry with you.' She thought it wrong that M should be denied children, so she suggested that her 'dear man' should 'see to it that one year M has a child and the next year I have a child, so you will always have a wife who is serviceable.' His wife, whom he always called 'Mutti' (little mother), wouldn't be 'serviceable' much longer; she was dying of cancer of the womb.

---

* In the middle of the war, in one of his greatest rabble-rousing speeches, Goebbels had shouted at his audience in Berlin, 'Wollt Ihr den totalen Krieg?' (Do you want total war?). Enthusiastically they had yelled back that they did. In the end the German people got it, and then some!

The former starlet, who now performed on the stage in East Germany, might have been of interest to the German and Allied authorities. For Bormann was still being actively sought all over the world and was, indeed, the number one on the West's list of missing war criminals. But what had she to do with exhumation of the body now supposedly lying beneath the freshly disturbed soil? What was Manja Behrens, as she was called, doing here? What was the connection between her, the mistress, Martin Bormann, the lover, and Müller? For it was 'our dear Father, Heinrich Müller, killed in action Berlin, May 1945' who was now about to be taken to that discreet little room at the back of the cemetery's administration complex. For the first time since the alleged Müller corpse had been registered on 15 December 1945 under the number 11706/45 at Berlin-Central's Registry Office (*Standesamt*) – by whom no one knew – it was going to be examined.

As we have already seen, a Walter Lueders had buried Müller single-handed in Berlin's old Jewish Cemetery on 17 September 1945 when he turned up at the Garnison Cemetery. How, as Berlin's Senior Attorney Neumann stated at the time, 'is completely obscure'. Thereafter we know that Müller's identity documents were sent to his wife in Munich, but they turned up there with his photos and other data removed; for what reason is not clear, though one can make a guess. Finally, long afterwards, on 1 July 1958 to be exact, 'a lady living in Berlin' (as the firm involved recorded) ordered the marble gravestone to be made by the local firm of Pelz. The 'lady living in Berlin' was Müller's long-term mistress.

It is clear, on the basis of the above, that there was something very fishy about the Müller burial. Why had he been transferred from one cemetery to another? Lueders, who had allegedly buried him, stated afterwards that he had sent the documents he'd found on the corpse, by which he had identified it, to 'Müller's relatives who lived in the neighbourhood of the Hallesche Tor (in Berlin)'. But that had to be a lie because Müller's relatives were in Munich where Frau Müller worked as a sales assistant. So why did Lueders lie? He had no answer to the investigators' queries. As for the former

169

Kripo officer, Leopold, who had definitely identified Müller on the basis of his war medals, he was long dead and couldn't answer any questions.

It seemed, therefore, to those of the spectators of the macabre scene who knew the detailed background of the Müller Case, that Manja Behrens was present because of her connection with Bormann in the last year of the war and that Bormann also had a connection with the vanished Gestapo chief. The former starlet was present to establish a link between these most prominent war criminals. Bormann's body had still not been found, although there were those like Naumann and Axmann who maintained he had been killed on the night of May 1/2 1945. Now the papers were full of accounts of how Bormann had escaped from Berlin and was being sighted by 'reliable witnesses' everywhere from Moscow to Miami.

Might the exhumation of the Müller corpse prove the contrary? At least the mouldering skeleton might give the investigators a clue to what had happened to Bormann that May night nearly two decades earlier.

But on that 25 September 1963 the investigators were doomed to disappointment. The worm-eaten wooden coffin was duly raised and opened to reveal a collection of bones and precious little else which might have given the investigators a clue as to whom the bones belonged. Under the direction of Berlin's *Oberststaatsanwalt* Neumann, they were taken to the Berlin Forensic Institute, directed by Professor Rommeney. He and his team went to work and came up with a big surprise. Some of the investigators had naturally expected that they wouldn't find Müller in the grave. By that time, especially in Germany, there were many who believed in the new-fangled conspiracy theories coming across the Atlantic. 'Chequebook journalism' was already flourishing and it helped those who might profit from such largesse to believe in the most impossible of plots. But not only were the bones not those of Müller, they were, as Professor Rommeney had proved by the end of September, those of *three* different and unknown persons!

In particular, the Professor ascertained that the skull in the

'Müller coffin' belonged to a 35-year-old man, whereas Müller would have been 45 if he had died in the supposed year of his death, 1945. The bones, too, were of men of various ages. It was clear that someone had prepared a fake corpse, carefully and deliberately. There had been skeletons a-plenty in Berlin in the summer of 1945. Thousands, according to the Red Army figures, had been killed there in the weeks of fighting. When it had all been over, the Russian authorities had ordered all corpses buried as soon as possible, without any great attention to detail or identification. The main thing, with water and sanitation facilities wrecked everywhere and thousands of Berliners living in cellars and ruins in the most primitive circumstances, was to avoid mass infections. At that time it wouldn't have presented difficulties for someone to dig up a corpse, or corpses, and use them for illegal purposes.

As the German magazine *Der Spiegel* commented at the time: 'If Gestapo Müller didn't really die in 1945 – and there are indications that he didn't – he has covered all the traces with a cunning that does all honour to his former profession. . . . There is no comparison between Müller's efforts and the clumsy hide-and-seek game which his subordinate Eichmann has played.'* The well-known German news magazine, which at times has researched such matters better than any police force or intelligence service, was right. But even the *Spiegel* could not make a guess at who had covered Müller's disappearance and obscured the trail, if he had really escaped from Berlin in May 1945. Nor could the magazine make a stab at where he might have gone. But one thing remained clear. Müller was back on the most wanted list once more. Throughout the West the security services were looking for 'Nazi War Criminal Number Two' yet again. Or were they?

* The Israelis had kidnapped Eichmann and brought him to trial three years before.

1945: FORTRESS IN THE ALPS.

'It would almost seem as though Allied Supreme Commander's intelligence staff had been infiltrated by British and American mystery writers.

William Shirer, *The Rise and Fall of the Third Reich*.

ONE

Back in the autumn of 1942, when the Red Orchestra crisis had reached its height in Berlin and Müller had learned that even upper-class people could betray their country to Moscow, a Munich businessman named Schmidhuber had been arrested entering Switzerland. He had risked the death penalty for attempting to smuggle foreign currency into that country. It was not an uncommon offence at a time when, as Müller expressed it contemptuously, the rats were beginning to leave the sinking ship. But Schmidhuber, a Bavarian businessman, was not just another rich man trying to rescue what he could while he had the chance or someone trying to hedge his bets with money in neutral Switzerland.

He was in fact an agent of the *Abwehr* and the foreign currency he had smuggled across the Swiss frontier had been intended for a group of German-Jewish refugees in that country. As soon as Müller heard the news, he felt that Schmidhuber's chief, Admiral Canaris, would make a move by which he would incriminate himself. But the ageing Canaris did nothing.

However, Schmidhuber, well aware of Müller's reputation back in the old days in Munich, decided to sing. And he had a lot to sing about. He told Müller and his other Gestapo interrogators that another member of the *Abwehr* had made a secret approach to the Vatican in 1940 in an attempt to secure peace. He revealed that a well-known German churchman, Dr Dietrich Bonhoeffer, had met the British Bishop of

Chichester in Stockholm on a similar mission. Again his passport had been provided by the *Abwehr*. He confessed, too, that the *Abwehr* had smuggled other Jewish families out of Germany into Switzerland, whether because their lives were in danger or as a result of bribes he didn't know. Slowly but surely he implicated Canaris. But there was not enough evidence for Müller to arrest the Admiral. However, there was more than enough for him to question two of Canaris' senior associates, von Dohnanyi and General Oster, the *Abwehr*'s Chief-of-Staff.

On 5 April 1943 Air Force Judge Manfred Roeder, who had played a key role in the recent sentencing of the Berlin Red Orchestra traitors, appeared with a Gestapo officer at Canaris' offices on the Tirpitzufer in Berlin. He asked to see von Dohnanyi.

With Canaris and Oster present, Roeder questioned the senior *Abwehr* man. Roeder rattled the *Abwehr* officer, but didn't get much out of him until he spotted von Dohnanyi attempting to palm a piece of paper and then shove it to Oster. Roeder at once demanded to see it. It was marked with a large 'O' in coloured pencil ('O' for Oster) and a list of what appeared abbreviated names, some crossed out. He couldn't make out what it meant, but he was sharp enough to realize that it had to be important if it made two middle-aged spymasters act like schoolboys cribbing in an exam. He ordered the arrest of von Dohnanyi and asked Canaris to suspend Oster from duty.

It seemed to take Müller and his officers a long time to decipher the 'O' and the scribbled, crossed-out initials. However, it was clear that Himmler didn't want to have Canaris arrested just yet. Indeed it took until February 1944 before Canaris was removed from office and given another job, which was really a sinecure, and Himmler set about amalgamating the *Abwehr* and the *SS-SD*, as Heydrich and Schellenberg had wanted two years earlier.

About this time an aristocratic giant of an officer arrived in Berlin. Once he had fought in Rommel's 10th Armoured Division against Patton in the last stages of the Northern African campaign. Now one-armed, one-eyed Colonel von

Stauffenberg, who the head of the German resistance against Hitler described as a 'cranky fellow . . . who wanted to steer a dubious course with the left-wing socialists and Communists and gave me a bad time with his overwhelming egotism', wanted put new life into the German right-wing plot to kill Hitler.

As all the world knows, the July 1944 bomb plot instigated by von Stauffenberg to assassinate the Führer at Rastenburg failed. Thereafter came the reckoning, and Müller was going to play a major role, his last one to be sure, in that reckoning. Many allowed themselves to be tamely butchered by their fellow officers before the Gestapo could get their hands on them. Others, the born survivors, who had played a double game for years, fled to nearby neutral countries. Only the brave and the fools stayed behind to face the music.

Canaris was naturally one of the first to be arrested. He would die in 1945, strangled by a length of chicken wire at Flossenburg Concentration Camp. But there were others.

One, in particular, perhaps the most surprising member of that plot to kill the Führer, stuck it out as long as possible, refusing to be panicked into making a run for it. Finally, however, the Gestapo, raking over every clue to find the traitors, who were located not only all over Germany but in the occupied territories as well (Rommel was one) turned back to that mysterious scrap of paper marked with an 'O' which had been seized at *Abwehr* HQ the previous year.

Their efforts to decipher the scrawled abbreviations produced the surprise of their lives. Oster had scribbled 'Schu', 'Gi' and 'Ne.' 'Schu' was Count von der Schulenberg, the former German Ambassador in Moscow; 'Gi,' Dr Hans Gisevius, a former Gestapo agent now working secretly with Allen Dulles, head of the American OSS in Switzerland, and 'Ne' was no other than Müller's old comrade SS General Artur Nebe, head of the *Kripo*.

Since the abortive assassination attempt Nebe had been playing the role of his life, going to the Gestapo HQ each day, eating lunch with colleagues such as Kaltenbrunner and Müller, and generally expressing his dismay that there should be such traitors in their midst. As one of his former colleagues noted, 'We all thought Nebe one of the best.'

Nebe was even instrumental in having one of the senior plotters arrested in the Prinz Albrecht Strasse by Müller himself. He invited his old friend Count Helldorf, an SS General and Chief of Police of Berlin, to visit him on 'an important matter'. Helldorf appeared and told Nebe, his fellow conspirator, 'A bold front is all that can help us now. . . . Just behave as though everything is fine.'

They chatted for a while and then the door was flung open and Gestapo men rushed in, pistols at the ready. 'You're under arrest.'

'Well, well,' Helldorf commented calmly as he confronted Müller, who had organized the arrest. He kept his mouth shut then, but Nebe knew Müller would make Helldorf talk. It was time to make a move.

A week later a couple bathing in the Wannsee Lake reported an abandoned Mercedes nearby. The car was quickly identified as Nebe's and for a while it was generally supposed that the Police Chief had committed suicide. Müller wasn't so sure. He put a senior detective in charge of the investigation. He told him, 'Himmler's getting angry. He says Nebe must be found.'

The inquiry took four months. Finally the detectives found a spurned former mistress of his who betrayed his whereabouts and Müller sent no fewer than twenty men to arrest his former colleague.

They brought him back to the recently bombed Gestapo HQ and Müller was surprised by his appearance, with his shabby clothes and dyed hair. Indeed it was said he hardly recognized the former dandy without his snappy SS uniform. Still Müller recovered quickly enough and ensured that Nebe's throat, mouth and anus were checked for poison capsules (this is the first mention of these 'L for Lethal' pills which were going to figure in the lives of the Nazi bigshots in the last months of the war). Then he told Nebe, 'You will understand that you are now *Herr* Nebe and no longer Artur to me.' Then he and Kaltenbrunner cross-examined him.

Three months later Nebe, who denounced many of the plotters, was taken to Buchenwald Concentration Camp and finally removed from there to be strangled in Berlin's Plotzensee Prison.

Müller's reaction is not recorded, but Nebe's downfall and execution must have been a salutory lesson even for him. Now he alone of those who had sat around the table with Himmler at the outbreak of the Second World War was still in power. Heydrich was dead; Naujocks had vanished and was supposed to be working for the British; Nebe had been executed. Might he not be next? He must have realized that he would have to do something soon if he wasn't to suffer the same fate as the others.

He would have been even more perturbed if he had known for sure that Naujocks was indeed in British hands. Even worse, he was now in that 'London Cage', where that benevolent old Colonel was questioning him.

Naujocks called the old man 'King of the Cage', but his real name was Colonel Alexander Scotland, head of the PWIS*, who had been in intelligence since the turn of the century. Benign as he looked, Naujocks later confessed that he 'felt a little afraid of this man'. And Naujocks was right to be afraid. A veteran of three wars, Scotland had seen service not only in the British Army, but in the German Forces too!

Back in 1903 the young Scot had been trying his hand at business in what was then German South-West Africa when the local Hottentots rose in revolt against their German colonial masters. In the four-year war that followed Scotland was given a German rank, uniform and weapon to protect himself as he supplied the German Army with goods and comforts. In the course of that forgotten war, he was approached by a British Intelligence officer and asked 'to keep an eye' on the Germans. It was his first contact with Secret Service work.

In 1914, still in South-West Africa, he was arrested by his former German friends as a spy. He escaped, made his way to London and there joined the Intelligence Corps. For a while he was engaged in routine Intelligence duties in France, trying to work out the enemy's order of battle. A year later,

* Prisoner of War Interrogation.

179

however, bored with staff work, he was given the task of running agents in the German-Dutch-Belgian frontier area. Here Holland bulges into Germany in the Maastricht area, the frontiers are difficult to control and the locals on both sides of the border speak German.

More than once Scotland, who spoke fluent German, ventured into German camps and barracks to listen to soldiers' gossip. In neutral Holland he ran the risk of being tossed into the nearest canal if he were caught by the opposition's agents.

When the war ended in 1919 Scotland thought he was finished with Intelligence, but he was mistaken. In the '20s, as a businessman often travelling to Germany, he was asked by the SIS at Queen Anne's Gate to keep his eyes and ears open and report on what he saw. In September 1939 it had seemed perfectly natural for the 60-year-old Scot to offer his services once again to 'the Old Firm' and they were eagerly accepted.

By late 1944 Scotland probably knew more about the *Wehrmacht* than many a German general. He had instituted the standard Red Cross form which every PoW used so that his next-of-kin could be informed that he was safe. Naturally he had introduced a few odd wrinkles into it in order to obtain information, and he had bugged cells, especially those of high-ranking German officers. Thus he'd heard General von Thoma tell a fellow general about Germany's secret missiles. He had tricked Franz von Werra, the first German PoW to attempt to escape from a British camp, and so on.

Now, in the autumn of 1944, he was working, among many other cases (especially a mysterious message that Ultra had picked up from Hitler's chief military adviser, Field Marshal Keitel), on the Great Escape. That was where Naujocks, who had deserted to the British in Belgium, came in. He knew the leading personalities of the Gestapo and *Kripo*, and who were involved in the murders, and he was prepared to tell Scotland everything he knew, but at a price.

Nebe had been ruled out by Naujocks, rightly so, as it turned out. For when Scotland finally assembled his witnesses in Hamburg for the Great Escape war crimes trial of 1946, one of his chief witnesses, the Prinz Albrecht Strasse clerk Hans

Merten related, 'When General Nebe was ordered by Himmler, "We will make it fifty" [ie recaptured PoWs to be shot], Nebe was "excited and uncontrolled" because he was aware of the monstrosity of the deed he was about to carry out.'

But there had to be others, Scotland reasoned. What about Müller, about whom the British already knew? What role had he taken in the murders? Slowly the net was beginning to close in on him. Those who knew the British knew they'd never forget Müller, whatever happened in the intervening months before the war ended in the Allied favour. To any intelligent observer in that cold autumn before Hitler made his one last desperate attempt to achieve victory in the West, or at least to win a more favourable peace for Germany, it was clear that Müller could certainly find no sanctuary in Britain.

TWO

Carl Johann Wiberg had been in business in Berlin for over thirty years, but in the spring of 1945 the middle-aged Swedish businessman had nothing to do. His glue factory had been completely destroyed by the great Allied raids of the late winter. All that seemed left to the 49-year-old widower – his wife had died in 1939 – was to take his pet dachshunds, Onkel Otto and Tante Effi for a walk.

Every morning he would prepare the two dogs on the balcony of his second-floor Berlin-Wilmersdorf flat, from which a couple of ropes always hung, then dress himself carefully in his immaculate topcoat and Homburg hat before setting off with the dogs through the bomb-shattered suburb.

Occasionally he would break his morning walk to go to his favourite *Kneipe* bar at the corner of the Nestorstrasse, where he would listen to the usual complaints and gossip of those around. The gossip was usually pretty accurate. For Harry Rosse's *Kneipe* was favoured by the local National Socialist bigwigs and *Wehrmacht* officers on duty in the capital. Sometimes he would patronise a special food shop which sold foodstuffs for foreign currency at very high prices without ration coupons. Here he would keep his ears open.

His morning walk completed, he would return to his apartment, which was always kept shuttered and barred. In due course he would receive his new Berlin girlfriend, Inge. He would brief the new love of his life on what to do if the Gestapo raided the flat. 'Through the apartment at the

182

double, on to the balcony and then down the ropes into the courtyard and off'.

For Carl Wiberg was an American spy, perhaps the only resident OSS agent in the whole of surrounded Berlin.

'Since I had lived over thirty years in Berlin and knew the old Germany, Hitler's acts after 1933 filled me with disgust,' Wiberg recalled years later. 'The war that Hitler provoked was the last straw for me. I began to hope that something would happen to free humanity from the Nazi régime and its servants. In addition, I had always felt the greatest admiration for the English and their democracy.'

Wiberg was in a way unique. Many educated Swedes seem to have wanted a German victory until 1943/44. Most Swedish export business was done with Germany which *was* fighting Sweden's battle against the Russians. (Almost to the end Sweden allowed German troop trains to and from the Eastern Front to pass through their territory.) In September 1944 Wiberg was called to Stockholm by a Dane in the same trade as himself, Hennings Jessen-Schmidt. But the Dane was no ordinary businessman. He was a leader of the Danish resistance and a member of the American Secret Intelligence organization, the OSS.

The two men talked for five solid hours. 'I was both surprised and shocked,' Wiberg recalled years afterwards. 'I realized the risk I was running and knew what would happen to me if I fell into the hands of the Gestapo. I asked for some time to think over his offer to spy for the USA in Berlin, though in reality I had already made up my mind that I might be able to make some small contribution to the end of this terrible war.'

Wiberg made his decision. Not only was he to spy at a low level, but he was also to be the OSS's 'storekeeper' in Berlin.

That winter strange individuals would arrive at his flat at all hours of the day and night to deliver goods 'from your friends in Stockholm'. By that spring of 1945 he had a variety of drugs and knockout drops in his flat, plus a suitcase full of high explosives, hidden temporarily in a rented garage until he found another, perfect, hiding place for the suitcase – the strong box in the vault of the local Deutsche Union Bank.

By the end of that winter Wiberg was becoming worried. He had thought that his assignment was to have been of a temporary nature, but now he was informed by his Danish spymaster that it didn't look as if the Anglo-Americans would be the first to enter Berlin after the crossing of the Rhine; it would be the Red Army. Unknown to Wiberg, Eisenhower's discovery of something called the 'Alpine Redoubt' in the Austro-Bavarian alps had changed the direction of the Allied attack. Instead of Berlin, the Anglo-Americans' main objective now was southwards into Bavaria and the Tyrol in Austria.

Then Wiberg had a stroke of luck. He was shopping in the special store when he heard a tremendous piece of news. Two well-dressed women whose husbands, Wiberg knew, were high-ranking Nazis, mentioned that Hitler was still in Berlin or the general area of the German capital. He hadn't fled or gone underground, as Allied Intelligence had suspected, after all.

But there was a snag. The radio transmitter which lay in parts in Wiberg's coal cellar had not yet been assembled. He and the Dane had to wait till a courier was found to take the news back to neutral territory and from there to Colonel David Bruce, OSS chief in London, and Paris. Finally the message was received at OSS HQ in Grosvenor Square and a decision made. On the afternoon of 12 April 1945 the nameless courier appeared at Wiberg's flat to inform him that Hitler had located his headquarters at the little town of Bernau some fourteen miles north-east of the capital.

Wiberg guessed that, as their armies couldn't get through to Berlin, the Western Allies would use bombers to 'liquidate' the Führer. He told his new friend Hennings Jessen-Schmidt, 'What better birthday present for the Führer on 20 April than a large-scale bombing raid.'*

The fact that the Americans possessed only one amateur agent in the German capital tells us two things: one, that Eisenhower was no longer interested in Berlin as his primary military objective; two, that Allied Intelligence, at least, *was*

---

* Hitler's birthday was on 20 April, in this case his last.

interested in Hitler! As we shall see, the men in London went to great lengths to eradicate the Führer at his supposed new HQ in Bernau.

Nevertheless, this Intelligence disinterest in Berlin and what was going on in the soon-to-be beleagured city makes it extremely hard to follow Müller's movements in those last weeks of the war.

In those crucial weeks Eisenhower, who seemingly was pursuing not only military but political objectives (President Roosevelt was dying and had lost virtual control of political policy, especially where Europe was concerned), was primarily concerned with what was happening at the other end of the crumbling Reich, still not occupied by the Allies. For he had come to believe the rumours first floated by the Swiss, who had economic reasons of their own for spreading these rumours, and then picked up and embellished by Dr Josef Goebbels, Minister of Propaganda.

It was the great final ruse of the 'Redoubt' – the Alpine fortress where, allegedly, the elite of the SS, paratroopers and *Werwolf* fanatics of the German underground resistance would hold out for years among the snowbound heights around Hitler's own 'Eagle's Nest'.

Of course we know now that the whole idea of this remote Alpine fortress which would simply swallow up American assault divisions was one of the last great deception plans of the war as far as the almost beaten Germans were concerned.

Early in January of that year the phone had rung at the SS-SD headquarters in Innsbruck. A *Hauptsturmbannführer* Wandel from Bregenz, where the Germans had a listening station, wanted to talk to the SS man in charge, *Sturmbannführer* Gontard. 'What's going on up there?' Wandel asked. 'Are you building an alpine fortification system or something?'

Gontard's reply was to ask his subordinate whether he'd been drinking. Wandel assured him that he had never been so serious in his life. 'We've just picked up a message from Dulles [located in Swiss Berne] saying that we Germans are building a tremendous fortification system in the Alps.'

Gontard listened carefully before he hung up. He was

going to pass on the details of this strange fortress to *Gauleiter* Hofer, who had his command post in Bolzano in the South Tyrol.

So Gontard was summoned to meet the most powerful Nazi in that area of the Reich. He knew that Hofer was not a man to tolerate fools gladly, but he told the *Gauleiter* what he had heard from Bregenz and waited for the storm. But it didn't come.

Slowly Hofer turned towards Gontard and exclaimed, 'That is the best idea that the *Amis* [Americans] have had in this war. That Alpine fortification business is going to be our salvation.' So started the deception which changed the whole course of the campaign in the West and helped to form the post-war political map of Europe until the end of the Cold War a decade ago.

Who was behind the great deception, Germans or Americans, or both, is not clear to this day. The Germans naturally had an interest in it. For many of their war criminals the Alpine Fortress would provide a convenient 'parking lot' before they disappeared. Their bankers and businessmen also found the area very convenient in relation to the gold and assets they had already, or soon would, deposit in Switzerland. As for Dulles, the Republican with his big business connections in both America and Germany, he could use the prospect of a long-drawn-out and costly campaign in the Alps to help gain better terms for Germany than those of the Jewish-Democrat Morgenthau Plan and ensure an Allied-controlled Central Europe as a surety for US assets there and a bulwark against communism. Eisenhower's motives are really not clear to this day.

However, a SHAEF Intelligence summary for 11 March 1945 makes it quite clear how seriously Eisenhower took the threat of the Alpine Redoubt. It read: 'Here, defended by nature and by the most efficient secret weapons yet invented, the powers that have hitherto guided Germany will survive to reorganize her resurrection; here armaments will be manufactured in bomb-proof factories, food and equipment will be stored in vast underground caverns and a specially selected corps of young men will be trained in guerrilla warfare so that a whole underground army can be fitted and directed to liberate Germany from the occupying forces.'

As Shirer said in his *Rise and Fall of the Third Reich*: 'It would almost seem as though the Allied Supreme Commander's intelligence staff had been infiltrated by British and American mystery writers.'

Be that as it may, the imaginary Alpine Redoubt came as a blessing in disguise for certain Germans in those last weeks of the war. It was an opportunity for top-ranking SS-SD, Gestapo and *Kripo* officials to have themselves posted to the site of the Führer's last-ditch stand. If they felt that they might well be accused of war crimes once the Allies caught up with them they made doubly sure that they were sent there. As soon as the Reich lost the war and they were relieved of their oath of loyalty to the Führer, which, surprisingly enough, many of them took very seriously, they could do a bunk.

Under the nominal command of Field Marshal Albert Kesselring, these war criminals ensured that they were sent south to Bavaria and Austria. Not surprisingly, many of them hailed from the region and were soon to put their local knowledge to good use.

Dr Kaltenbrunner was one of the first to leave Berlin. He set up his headquarters in Alt-Aussee, soon to be the centre of the Nazi fugitives. Eichmann followed for a while, before disappearing on his own secret odyssey. He was joined by Dr Hoettl, longtime head of the SD in Southern Europe, who stayed in Alt-Aussee and died in bed there nearly fifty years later. Berger, the brain behind the *Waffen SS* was next, and so it went on, with war criminals, big and small, flocking to what would soon be a German enclave surrounded by Anglo-American troops advancing from Italy and Bavaria.

With them and after them came the treasures of the Reich, some bartered for worthless marks, some stolen, some extracted from the dying wretches in the concentration camps and some, surprisingly enough, German-owned, the treasures of centuries of German artistocratic collecting. They, in their turn, would be looted. But this time the looters would be Americans, with an eye for a good 'souvenir' when they saw it and thieves and black marketeers who flocked into the area.

But, again, what of Müller? Why did he stay in Berlin? Now that Himmler, Schellenberg and Kaltenbrunner had gone their separate ways he was in charge of the Security Service, if not in name, then in practice. There was, therefore, no one in authority save the Führer himself, and he had other problems, to make him stay in a capital that was soon to be virtually surrounded and was being bombed on a regular basis. Even his Prinz Albrecht Strasse HQ had been wrecked by US bombs.

He was a Bavarian through and through. He had a wife and children and relatives in Munich and in the surrounding countryside. There were only a few photos of him available and he was the senior Gestapo man, and senior war criminal, still in Berlin. He could easily have followed the others to the so-called 'Alpine Redoubt' and 'taken a dive'. The writing was on the wall for anyone to read and Müller knew it. So why didn't he flee before the Russians came? When they did, he would be one of the first to be arrested by his counterparts in the NKVD. What kept him in Berlin?

THREE

Adolf Hitler rose at eleven o'clock on the morning of his sixty-fifth birthday. Eva Braun, soon to be Frau Hitler, presented him with a portrait of herself in a jewelled silver frame. A short time later Martin Bormann made his usual daily appearance. He brought roses for the Führer.

Between eleven and twelve that morning the inner clique all paid their respects – Speer, Doenitz, soon to be the Führer's short-term successor, Ribbentrop, Keitel, Jodl, Himmler. Some had come from their hiding places, a few from their duty stations and one, 'my loyal Heinrich' (as Hitler always called Himmler) from his treacherous peace negotiations with Count Folke Bernadotte.

Someone discovered a pre-war gramophone. The birthday group drank champagne and settled down to listen to the only record they could find: a popular little movie tune of that year: *'Blutrote Rosen erzaehlen dir vom Glueck'* (Blood-Red Roses Tell You of Happiness).

Schellenberg, who happened to be in Berlin that morning, had toasted the Führer's health the night before with Himmler. Now, as he shaved, he heard the boom-boom of flak in the distance: the Americans, he assumed, back for one of their daytime raids on the capital. He was wrong. It was the RAF. But as he finished shaving he forgot the enemy *Terrorflieger* and presumably the Führer too. For he knew from a telephone call made by Himmler, who was now a pawn in Schellenberg's hands, that they were going to have to meet

189

Bernadotte on the morrow. Himmler would meet him at six in the morning in the remote country house they had selected for their talks. It was very risky, but it was Himmler's last hope of rescuing something from the mess.

In the event Himmler would learn from the Count that he was finished. As Bernadotte told Schellenberg before meeting Himmler: 'The *Reichsführer* no longer understands the realities of his situation. I cannot help him any more. He should have taken Germany's affairs into his own hands after my first visit. Now I can hold out little chance for him. And you, my dear Schellenberg, you would be wiser to think of yourself.'

It was unnecessary advice. The young general had always 'thought of himself'. He was a born survivor. Soon he would flee to neutral Sweden, taking his dark secrets with him, leaving his masters to their fates. 'For the time being,' as he wrote in the '50s after he had been released from an Allied jail, 'my services were not required.'*

That morning Jessen-Schmidt and Wiberg, America's men in Berlin, prepared to witness the death of Adolf Hitler. They were dressed in smart business suits and were now crouched in a field outside the supposed site of Hitler's HQ. Here they waited for the drama to begin.

They didn't have to wait long. Twin-engined British bombers came winging in, low and dead on time, from their field in Continental Europe. The 88 flak cannon hammered away, but the RAF pilots were not to be deflected from their attack on Bernau. Time and again they came roaring in, despite the anti-aircraft shells, to drop their bombs. Finally they disappeared, leaving behind a smoking, burning town. Some time later, as the two OSS agents prepared to leave, confident that the Führer *had* to be dead or at least badly wounded, a flight of Stormovik dive-bombers from the Red Army came in to continue the attack. They assumed that OSS Colonel Bruce in London had thought the attack on Bernau

* They never were. Thoroughly vetted and censored by the SIS, he was allowed to publish one book on his wartime exploits and then died, barely middle-aged, in 1952, in Italian exile.

190

so important that he had told the Russians of Hitler's supposed presence there.

He hadn't, but it didn't matter. The next day Jessen-Schmidt and Wiberg discovered that Hitler hadn't been in Bernau after all. Thereafter Wiberg had little time for OSS work. He was too busy dealing with marauding Russians out for loot, Schnapps and women. Indeed, a couple of days later Wiberg was identifying himself as an American spy to a Red Army Colonel when he heard his fiancée, also named Müller, screaming hysterically for help. A Russian officer had torn away most of her clothes and with the flies of his baggy breeches already open was trying to rape the terrified German girl. The liberators had arrived!

Thereafter, now that the Western Allies knew their plot to assassinate Hitler in Bernau had failed, Anglo-American Intelligence seemed to lose interest in what was happening in the German capital. Perhaps circumstances forced their hand. By now the Americans had linked up with the Russians at Torgau on the River Elbe and by the end of the month the British under Montgomery had crossed that river and were linking up with the Red Army at Wismar on the Baltic coast. An 'Iron Curtain', as Dr Goebbels had already called it prior to Churchill's famous utterance, was descending on Central Europe. It would be June before the Russians allowed their erstwhile Anglo-American allies, plus the French, to enter Berlin. Till then what was happening to the top Nazis would remain a closed book to Western Intelligence.

In embattled Berlin they thought they knew what was going on at the top level. At the time the traditionally big-mouthed Berliners* called what began on 20 April 1945 'the flight of the golden pheasants'. The 'golden pheasants' were the Party bigshots in their fancy uniforms, laden with gold braid. Now officers, officials and bureaucrats fled the capital before the Red Army took over what was left of unoccupied Berlin and made them pay for the fat years.

* The Berliners have always been celebrated in the rest of Germany for their fast speech and lack of respect for authority. *'Berliner Schnauze'* (Berlin Big Trap) the Germans still call it.

Even though Dr Goebbels had ordered, 'No man capable of bearing arms is to leave Berlin,' no one stopped them. In that week the Berlin Commandant's office issued two thousand permits to leave the capital. Colonel Hans Refior of that office later recalled: 'Despite Goebbels' order, we put no difficulties in the way of these "home fighters" (*Heimatkrieger*, here used ironically) who wanted passes. Why should we hold up these contemptible characters? They all believed that flight would save their precious lives. The rest remained behind. Flight for them was beyond their means anyway because of the transport difficulties.'

So by about 22 April most of the *Prominez* had fled the Führer Bunker, but Hitler and Goebbels were going to remain there for good. They were, as we are now aware, intent on committing suicide. As Hitler stated shortly before he killed Frau Hitler and himself, *he* was not prepared to be locked in a cage like a circus animal to be prodded by a howling enemy mob.* Two others, who ranked just below Hitler and Goebbels as likely candidates for trial as alleged war criminals, Martin Bormann and Heinrich Müller, were still there.

Yet it is clear from eyewitness accounts then and those later recorded by Hugh Trevor-Roper (Lord Dacre) in his semi-official enquiry, later published as *The Last Days of Hitler*, that neither were going to die in the Bunker. They were going to make a run for it.

But was Müller still in the Bunker, as was Bormann, after the Führer committed suicide? It seems there were no further sightings of Müller after he had taken General Fegelein away to be executed. SS General Rattenhuber, who was most closely associated with Müller at the time of the Fegelein Affair, seems to have spent his remaining time in the Bunker getting drunk. In the end, when the hour of the great breakout occurred, he pulled himself together and commanded one of the ten separate breakout parties. He was captured.

Speer, on the other hand, does mention Müller's presence

---

* Even now no one is quite sure how Hitler really met his end and what happened to his body. The recent Russian exhibition of Bunker artefacts and part of Hitler's alleged skull seem suspect to the experts.

in the Bunker afterwards. Hitler's one-time favourite and Minister of Armaments told American writer James O'Donnell: 'During my last visit to the Bunker on April 23 and 24, I recall Hitler mentioning that he had called in both Ernst Kaltenbrunner and Gestapo Chief Heinrich Müller . . . to make a thorough probe of Bunker internal security. . . . But Müller was in the Bunker to the very end.' In Speer's opinion, 'He was not normally a member of the Hitler inner circle. He was there because he had one specific job to do.'

Speer, who had twenty years in Spandau to talk about the events of that time, clearly states that Müller remained in the Bunker. His statement is backed up until 29 April by the others who worked together with him on the Fegelein affair. But what reason would he have to stay on after Hitler's death, now that Fegelein had been dealt with? He must have heard the others saying that as soon as the Führer took his own life – and they were sure he would – they would leave the Bunker and try to break out through the Russian lines. He had been called to the Bunker solely to solve the problem of the leak. Why not now return to his temporary headquarters in the basement of the *Dreifaltigkeitskirche*, or his mistress's home, perhaps even the little underground nest that Eichmann had prepared for himself for this eventuality, if the first two were now too dangerous?

These would have been safer options for a powerful man still having the backing of a police force and a spy organization. In a crisis Müller, who always played his cards close to his chest, probably knew he would be able to travel faster and further by himself.

But, before we go any further, it is of relevance to look at the great breakout from the Bunker after Hitler's death.

1946: END RUN

'I have no premonition of death. On the contrary, my burning desire is to live.'

Martin Bormann to his wife, Gerda, February, 1945.

ONE

In the bunker the leaders of the various escape groups were giving out their final instructions. There were approximately ten 'collectives', under the overall direction of 35-year-old General Moehnke of the *Waffen SS*. As soon as darkness fell on this May day they would begin their breakout between 8.45 and 10 pm. Group One, under Moehnke personally, would head for the nearest subway station and then walk along the railtracks in comparative safety until they reached the mainline station at Friedrichstrasse. Here they'd face the most dangerous part of their escape, or so they thought. For once out in the open they'd have to run the gauntlet of the Russian barrage, break through the Russian front and cross the River Spree. Once over the river, they'd probably have a chance of reaching the new Führer's headquarters (Admiral Doenitz) in Flensburg near to the Danish border.

Now, shortly after his adjutants had poured petrol over the bodies of Goebbels and his wife, who had just committed suicide*, Moehnke's party emerged from the Bunker. Most of them hadn't been above ground for at least three days and they were shocked by what they saw – a sea of smoking ruins, illuminated here and there by the lingering light of a Very flare or a Russian shellburst.

---

* The Goebbels poisoned their own children, but Harald Quandt, Goebbels' stepson, was in British captivity and would later buy BMW.

But they had no time to reflect on what had happened to Berlin. Time was of the essence. They crawled through a narrow hole in the Chancellery ruins near the corner of the Wilhelmstrasse (Berlin's Whitehall). Then, in single file, secretaries and soldiers, including Hitler's vegetarian cook and an admiral, they ran through the rubble for two hundred metres till they reached the ruined Hotel Kaiserhof opposite the entrance to the subway. Moehnke counted the men and women of his group, then ushered them down the steps of the subway.

The first group of escapers was underway. By midday on Wednesday, 2 May the 150 or so under the SS General's command reached a German SS tank unit. There they pulled out the bottles of spirits they had secreted about their persons and drank them. Even the twenty odd women with the party did the same, as Dr Schenk, the medical specialist from Aachen who had volunteered to stay with the SS wounded in the Bunker, testified later. Then a 'sergeant of the *Waffen SS*, who seemed to know the area,' volunteered to lead the women to safety, 'while the rest went on to meet their fate.*

Of the women who had followed Moehnke and then the unknown SS NCO, only one failed to make it. Hitler's and Bormann's secretaries both did, the latter, Else Kruger, turning up a few years later in, of all places, Cambridge, England. The one who didn't make it was Hitler's cook, Frau Konstanze Manzialy, an Austrian like her master.

Had she been killed? Gerda Christian, the wife of a *Luftwaffe* general and one of Hitler's prettier secretaries, spoke later about the Austrian peasant woman: 'I saw Fraulein Manzialy . . . disappear through a gaping hole in the brick wall. . . . I went to look for her and I called out, not too loudly perhaps. No answer. She had vanished. We never saw her again. But I heard no nearby shot, no scream, saw no one

---

* Schenk and Moehnke both became Soviet PoWs, spending nearly a decade in Russian hands. Here they were questioned time and again about Hitler and what had happened in the Bunker. Obviously the Russians, who captured it and presumably found Hitler's body, were unsure and wanted eye-witness accounts.

else about.' Frau Christian concluded, 'I had a hunch she might have just taken off on her own.'

So Moehnke suffered only one casualty, at least among the women in his party. He does not mention Müller being in his party. Neither does the other eye witness, Dr Schenk, who, like Moehnke, survived into the 1990s. So can we conclude that, *if* Müller had been in the Bunker and *had* broken out with the group most likely to succeed, he followed Fräulein Manzialy's example and quietly faded into the mass of civilians now drifting about a ruined Berlin?

At ten o'clock on the night of the breakout the Moehnke group was followed by that led by Dr Naumann, an assistant to Dr Goebbels and a fervent Nazi who would be arrested by the British almost ten years later for allegedly attempting to start a new Nazi Party and the man to whom Müller, if he was there, would have been most likely to attach himself. For shortly before Naumann left, Bormann approached him and asked if he could come along. Naumann agreed and told Bormann, dressed now in the uniform of an SS General, 'Keep close to me.' Bormann, if we are to believe Schellenberg and Hoettl, was by now working to the same end as Müller himself. Therefore, the Naumann group would have been his most likely choice.

Carrying Hitler's last will and testament, which supposedly he would use at Doenitz's HQ, if he got through, to legitimize his claim to a post in any government the Admiral might form, Bormann left the Bunker with the fatalistic words, 'Well then, goodbye. I don't think there's much sense in it. I'll try though, but I don't think I'll get through.'

Colonel Erich Kempka, Hitler's SS driver, had already managed to get his group out of the Bunker and was about to cross the River Spree when they were hit by a sudden Russian artillery barrage. He shouted for his group to run for the shelter of the ruins at the Admiral Palace Theatre. By this time it was two o'clock on the morning of 2 May. Now as the barrage ceased, Kempka crept out of the theatre ruins to decide what he should do next.

A terrible sight met his gaze. In front of him lay the Weidendamm Bridge across the Spree. Beyond there was a rough-and-ready tank barrier. As he recorded later, 'I could hear several shots echoing hollowly. Otherwise the place was as still as death.' He knew that death was probably waiting for him and his group on the other side of that barrier. The dead lying sprawled all around told him that.

On his own he advanced to a handful of young SS troopers crouched on his side of the barrier. They told him that the street ahead was full of Russians. He chanced a look over the barrier. At the end of the Friedrichstrasse a huge bonfire was blazing. Its purpose was obvious. The enemy were keeping it burning so that anyone who advanced beyond the barrier would become a perfect target, outlined against the flames. Dismayed, he retreated to his group.

Standing in the theatre's battered doorway, Kempka knew he'd have to make a decision soon. In May dawn came early. Suddenly his heart skipped a beat. A small group of figures in uniform was making its way in his direction. They were in single file and hugged the houses as if they were expecting trouble. His finger curled around the trigger of his pistol. Were they Russians? Then he recognized their uniform. They were Germans. Now, as the little file came closer, he saw who they were. In the red glow reflected from the Russian bonfire he recognized them as former inmates of the Bunker. In front came Bormann in a brown leather coat, then Dr Stumpfegger, one of Hitler's several doctors. Behind him was the one-armed Hitler Youth Leader Axmann. A few more and then Baur, Hitler's elderly pilot, but not a mention of Müller.

An hour later they were on their way again, the two groups joined together. They came upon a burning Tiger tank. Suddenly all hell was let loose. Russian shells came raining down. They had been spotted.

Still they pushed on. By this time they were approaching the Lehrter Station, which they guessed was already behind the Russian lines. It was, and there was an unpleasant surprise waiting for them there – the Russians – and they had spotted the escaping Germans! Still they didn't shoot them out of hand, as they might have done under the circumstances. For they were drunk and celebrating. They called to the advancing Germans, '*Voina kaput*' (war finished).

200

Now in a mixture of German, Russian and gestures, they talked and smoked coarse black Russian *marhoka* tobacco, rolled into newspaper to make a crude cigarette. Axmann, who had lost his arm in Russia, showed the delighted Russian captors how his artificial arm worked!

But Axmann saw danger ahead. He had just spotted 'Bormann, followed by Stumpfegger, leave the group and begin to steal away, hurrying into the shadows, taking off in the direction of the Invalidenstrasse.'

It took the Russians only a few moments to spot them. 'They became distrustful,' Axmann recalled after the war, 'and we felt a sense of danger about what might happen to us now.' Axmann decided he'd better get out of harm's way as well and, feeling there was no other way out, he joined the others. So four of them, Naumann, Axmann and two of the adjutants slipped away in the same direction.

Although the Russians they had just left had declared the war over, others obviously didn't agree. The Germans were abruptly struck by a furious barrage. Bullets scythed through the air. Axmann had lost the others, save an adjutant named Weltzin. These two braved the barrage, dodging from doorway to doorway until, suddenly, they stopped.

In front of them, on the little shell-pocked bridge which ran over the railtracks leading from the Lehrter Station, Axmann, in the lead, saw two figures sprawled out as if dead. Were they men from their own group? He ran forward, followed by Weltzin.

'We knelt at their side,' Axmann remembered. 'Perhaps we could help them. They were Martin Bormann and Dr Stumpfegger. Any mistake is ruled out. I could see their faces quite clearly. They lay on their backs, arms and legs stretched out. I touched Bormann. No reaction. I bent over him and could not trace any sign of breathing. I couldn't see any sign of blood or wounds.' Had they taken poison?

But the two had no time to answer that question, which would occupy the attentions of at least two generations of investigators. Russian sharpshooters were zeroing in on them. Bullets were bouncing off the stonework on both sides of them. It was not safe to stay there any longer. As an ancient

Russian machine gun joined in the fire, Axmann and Weltzin ran for their lives. In moments they had vanished into the darkness.

Allied investigators long doubted Axmann's testimony. After all he was an ardent Nazi who had corrupted Germany's youth when he had been the head of the *Hitler-Jugend* organization. Why should he tell them the truth?

Yet whether Axmann did or did not spot the dead Bormann that night, and I think he did, does not concern us in this context. What does is the fact that Axmann had been in the Bunker. Indeed he was intimately acquainted with all the leading Nazis there, including Müller. Yet he did not mention him once in his testimony, which was checked and re-checked by Allied and German authorities right up until the time that Bormann was officially pronounced dead by the West German government in 1972.

Over nearly twenty years of intense interrogation, Müller's name never cropped up. Neither did it in the post-war testimonies of the others who survived the breakout from the Bunker – Moehnke, Baur, Frau Christian, Naumann and the rest.

So can we assume that, if Müller was in the Bunker after Hitler committed suicide, as Speer said he was, he didn't join the breakout? Here, however, we must recall that Speer himself had left the Bunker nearly a week before. So we must ask ourselves where was Müller on 1 May 1945?

TWO

The obvious answer is Berlin. Whether he was in the Bunker or not, and I think that all the available evidence shows he was not, he surely decided to remain in the capital.

Why? Because here he had his power base. The world of the Gestapo was admittedly falling apart, but some of its officials were remaining at their posts. What else could they do? Besides, in the last hours of the Reich soldiers and officials who abandoned their posts were being shot out of hand by SS 'Flying Tribunals'.* In other words, as long as Müller stayed on in the capital he still had men he could command to do his bidding.

Müller had once been a soldier, too. He had experienced the confusion and breakdown of the Imperial Army in France at the end of the First World War. Although he had been only a teenager then, he had probably learned from that experience that it was only hotheads and fools who acted before the situation had been clarified a little.

Naturally he knew that the Russians would take Berlin. He'd know, too, that the Anglo-Americans had closed up along the western bank of the River Elbe, there to meet the Russians advancing from the east. In Central Germany and, to some extent, in his native Bavaria, the Allies had made

---

* Three-officer courts who charged, tried and usually shot or hanged supposed traitors, deserters and defeatists in a matter of minutes.

203

deep penetrations, but had not yet linked up with the Red Army advancing through Czechoslovakia and Eastern Austria. He would have known that too. For German staffs were still using a system of communication and local intelligence that has never really been assessed by researchers into this confused period of German history.* It was the *Reichspost* telephone system. Whereas many of their male colleagues took to their heels, a number of the women employed by the Third Reich's postal system remained at their posts, in particular the young telephonists manning the exchange systems.

They could always be tapped from Berlin – the system was working right to the very end – to discover whether the enemy had yet arrived in a particular town. Any senior German officer who had the power to do so could, within reason, discover what was going on, even behind enemy lines.

It is possible, too, that Müller now knew the details of the Anglo-American top-secret plan for Germany once the final phase of the Third Reich's collapse had been reached. 'Operation Eclipse', as it was code-named, had been in Germany's possession since at least January 1945. General Student, head of the German 1st Parachute Army, claimed that his people had captured the plan from the British in Holland. Colonel-General Jodl, Hitler's chief-of-operations, maintained that it had been discovered in the wreckage of a shot-up British armoured car during the final stages of the Battle of the Bulge. Neither explanation seems likely. What would frontline troops be doing carrying into battle a plan which detailed Allied intentions for a defeated Third Reich? After all, it included the future of Berlin, the division

---

* When for instance, the German 7th Army retreated through the German border country towards the Rhine in late March 1945, its chief-of-staff, von Gersdorff, followed the rate of the American advance by calling local German female operatives and asking them to report. Bravely they did so, risking the fact that they might well have been shot as spies by Patton's men.

† Later a French zone of occupation was agreed upon, making four zones in all.

of Germany into three zones[*], and much else. The 'Eclipse' plan was of the greatest political and military magnitude.

At all events, if Müller knew of 'Eclipse' (and seemingly many high-ranking Germans did and used the knowledge to evacuate their families and assets out of the future Russian Zone and into the supposedly safer western ones), he would know the details of the new zonal frontiers. Thus by 1 May he would have been in a position to select the zone in which he would feel safest. In addition, thanks to the telephone exchange system, he'd be able to find out where the enemy troops would be in the individual zones on any given day. He might be trapped in Berlin, but he wasn't blind; he knew how to escape from the trap.

So what could he do with this knowledge? There are four possibilities: (1) Stay in hiding in Berlin and wait to see which way the wind blew when the fighting was over; (2) Take the route attempted by the Moehnke group westwards and try to reach the Admiral Doenitz enclave in still-unoccupied Schleswig-Holstein; (3) Make for his native heath, in particular the supposed 'Alpine Fortress'; (4) Surrender to the Western Allies and hope that he could barter his knowledge of the Nazi top brass and/or communist networks already in existence in Germany.

Berlin, the first option, might appear to have been the most dangerous. Surely, one might ask, the Russians would be the first to take their revenge on the Germans who had devastated their land, killing an estimated twenty million Soviet citizens.

The contrary, however, was the case. The Russians, unlike the Western Allies, did not pursue the leading Nazis on the same systematic basis as the British and Americans. Naturally they had their secret police, the dreaded NKVD, out in full force in their part of occupied Germany. There were whole battalions of them. But they seemed to be more concerned with apprehending the many renegade Russians who had served in the German Army, 600,000 of them, as auxiliaries or in the four Cossack divisions.

Perhaps, too, the Russians thought that Müller and his Gestapo were little different from their own cruel authorities, who sent whole populations, such as the Volga Germans, into Siberian exile or to the gulags.

For a while the Russian Zone of Occupation and Berlin, still totally under Russian control till mid-June 1945, was certainly a viable option for Müller. But what about the 'Doenitz Enclave', based on Schleswig-Holstein? Here, from his naval HQ at Flensburg, Admiral Doenitz and his 'cabinet'* ruled over the area and the approximately two million German service personnel who had surrendered to the British but were administering themselves. Would this be a safe refuge for the fugitive until the time came for him to move on? Himmler was then in that area, disguised as a sergeant in the German Field Security Police and still not apprehended.

Müller knew little of the British, yet he had heard that the 'English gentlemen' would stop at nothing and had long memories. The future meant little to them; they lived in the past and remembered accordingly. Hadn't the Jewish poet Heine once said, when asked where he would like to die: 'England, because there everything happens a hundred years later than anywhere else'. Would they still be looking for him in London on account of the 'Commando Order' and the 'Great Escape' shootings? They would.

By now Colonel Scotland was well advanced into his investigation of the 'Great Escape' murders. He had used his well-honed technique of interrogation to get his prisoners to talk. He had played off one against the other, employed the old 'sweet-sour' treatment and by the time the war ended he had eight Germans from the Prinz Albrecht Strasse HQ of the Gestapo in custody, though, as he commented afterwards, 'It soon became plain that I was dealing with a collection of pompous arrogant Prussians, who had been little more than office stooges'.

All the same one of these 'office stooges' turned out to be a find. The odd man out was a short amiable Bavarian called Peter Mohr, a civilian prisoner, who held the rank of *Kriminal-*

---

* Doenitz lived in cloud-cuckoo land, as did his 'cabinet'. They were still discussing who would occupy the 'Ministry of Churches' when the British came to arrest them in their 'schoolroom' cabinet office.

kommissar in the Berlin *Kripo* under General Nebe. His job appeared to include a good deal of liaison work with Gestapo officials. Mohr started to spill the beans and, one by one, Scotland began to find out the names of the killers.

But he wanted more than just the murderers, his primary objective. 'We wanted the "head office boys" from Berlin, the executives and administrators.' And by now Scotland knew that the main 'head office boy' was none other than Müller.* It was clear that there'd be no sanctuary for him in the 'Doenitz Enclave'.

For Müller, however, probably hiding in Eichmann's bolt-hole in Berlin's Kurfürstenstrasse, there remained the flight of some 300 miles to the Alpine Redoubt area. Between Berlin and the Bavarian frontier with Austria, now soon to be 'liberated' from its Nazi occupiers, the military situation was still very fluid.

The Americans had not yet taken Berchtesgaden. Indeed, they seemed more concerned with the prestige object of stopping the French Army beating them there than capturing the area. In Central Germany, east of the Elbe, there were large enclaves still nominally under German control, or at least where the Allies had not yet arrived and taken over.

Müller would have known, as long as he kept in radio contact with Kaltenbrunner in Alt-Aussee, Austria, how many of his fellow fugitives had arrived in the area and were 'waiting for further processing'. If he could survive the 300-mile trek from pocket to pocket of German-held territory without being apprehended, he might have thought he had a chance. There was also the possibility that he might be able to do a deal with certain Americans, those who put political expediency before morality.

For Müller had long been aware that there were certain

---

* It took Scotland nearly two years to bring the Gestapo killers to trial in Hamburg. Fourteen of the eighteen accused were hanged. However, Scharpwinkel, the Gestapo Chief of Breslau, a main suspect, escaped because he was in a Moscow prison and the Russians wouldn't release him. According to Scotland, he was still alive somewhere in Russia or East Germany ten years after his comrades had been executed.

people not only in von Ribbentrop's Foreign Ministry who were having discussions with Allen Dulles, America's head of the OSS in Berne, but also right at the top in the SS. General Wolff, Himmler's liaison officer in Italy, had been instrumental in bringing about the independent capitulation of the German 10th Army in Italy to the Anglo-Americans in secret talks held with Dulles in neutral Switzerland. Perhaps, in exchange, for his knowledge of international Soviet communism, Dulles, who had a phobia about a communist-dominated Central Europe, might be prepared to do a deal with him. So was this the option that Müller finally took in the first week of May 1945 – an escape to his native Bavaria with its border with nearby Switzerland conveniently located for an approach to Mr Dulles?

Naturally the reasoning is conjectural. But there are witnesses who stated afterwards that Müller had told them he didn't intend to wait for the Russians to apprehend him. He knew what they would do if they got their hands on him. Contrary to the statements of Schellenberg, Gehlen, Hoettl and the rest (remember these statements were made at the start of the Cold War when any German blackening the Russians would be gratefully patted on the head and suitably rewarded regardless of his past crimes) Müller made his position quite clear as early as 2 May 1945.

According to one Dr Helmut 'K', he met Müller at one-thirty on that day. Müller had returned to the Bunker hospital, together with SS *Sturmbannführer* Scheedle. He had come to visit one of his officers, Wilhelm Bock, who had been badly wounded in the fighting and now had poisoned himself rather than fall into enemy hands. He looked at the corpse and, apparently satisfied with what he had seen, turned to go. Dr K, a dentist, working as an emergency doctor, asked Müller and his companion if they wanted to stay in the Bunker. Müller replied, 'I'm not going to let myself be strung up by the Russians.'

This ties in with his statement to Hitler's pilot, Hans Baur, on the previous evening at around seven o'clock as the escape parties were assembling, that 'We [presumably he meant the men of the Gestapo] know the Russian methods. . . .

I wouldn't place myself in the danger of landing in Russian imprisonment.'

Perhaps, with his detailed knowledge of those Russian methods, Müller already knew that, although they were not generally interested in supposed German war criminals, there was a special branch of the NKVD interested in one particular group of Germans. This was *Smersh* (Death Group), against which '007' was always pitted in Ian Fleming's James Bond adventures. The *Smersh* men were already in Germany seeking those *Abwehr* and Gestapo officers who had been involved in the detection and destruction of the Red Orchestra. As one of the Gestapo officials involved, Heinz Pannwitz, who had worked the Paris end of the 'radio game' and was now a prisoner of the Russians, recalled after his release in the early '50s: 'One of the first things the Russian Smersh people asked me was where is *Obergruppenführer* Müller?' Obviously Müller, who had used captured Red Orchestra 'pianists' to relay false information to the Soviets until the very end in April 1945, would be a prime target.* Müller knew, too, that the Russians would stop at nothing, including torture, to get the information they required if he ever fell into their hands.

Be that as it may, the last valid witnesses to speak to Müller on the evening and night of 2 May 1945 reported that he was calm but resigned. Rattenhuber, who was about to make a run for it with his remaining subordinates from the Hitler Bodyguard, noting that Müller was wearing a Walther PPK pistol, called across to him, 'Well Heinrich, what gives? We're going. It's high time.' According to Rattenhuber, Müller replied, 'No, Hans, the government's fallen and I fall with it.'

A little later Müller came across Paul 'E', a member of the Gestapo unit which had been commanded by William Bock, who had just committed suicide in the Bunker hospital. The young man asked quietly, 'What are we going to do now,

---

* Some of those who suspected Müller of being a Soviet agent maintain that he used this radio game with the Russians to relay valid information to Moscow instead of the half-truths and lies which usually make up that kind of double-dealing.

Gruppenführer? Are we going to manage it?' Müller shrugged, as if it didn't really matter. He replied, in rough working-class German, *'Nee, ich hau' nicht ab!'* ('No, I'm not doing a bunk').

Yet when the next senior officer of the Bock group, Christian 'W', asked Müller who was with his long-time associate Scholz, the same question, he answered, 'Let's wait and see.' Scholz, one of the last to see Müller, just smiled.

THE MÜLLER FILE
FOUR

After nearly a quarter of a century as a journalist and writer Ladislas Farago, the Hungarian-American writer, had by the late '60s finally made it with his book on General George S. Patton. Made into a movie with George S. Scott as Patton, the celebrated film brought the author fame and fortune. It was said that in the blackest days of Vietnam President Nixon saw the movie time and again in order to give himself courage to continue the fight.

By the early seventies, however, Farago turned to his old love – espionage and the Nazi period. Now he could command large advances, including one from the London *Daily Express*, which in due course became the main mouthpiece for his extraordinary, and, in the end, embarrassing findings. For Farago had decided to 'search the world' for the missing war criminals. Unlike the two most celebrated 'Nazi Hunters' of that period, Simon Wiesenthal and Beate Klarsfeld, his search was no crusade. Instead the now popular American writer said that his intention was more down-to-earth, almost sociological. As he wrote at the time, 'Although the vast majority of Nazi criminals live in Germany . . . my interest was pre-empted by those who chose to escape and start a new life.'

Naturally his main interest was in the 'names' who had escaped or were still not accounted for, and, as Eichmann had been discovered by the Israeli *Mossad* in South America, it was to that continent that he turned his attention. But first

213

Farago had to work out how the these top Nazis had escaped to the other side of the world; the organizations which had helped them at the beginning in 1945/46 and the routes – the 'ratlines', as the professional Nazi hunters and their journalist friends were calling them – they had taken from Occupied Germany to the various 'exit' ports, mainly Italian.

Farago chose Müller as his first target. For some reason, the Israelis had not bothered with him, save on one occasion of which we will hear more later. Simon Wiesenthal, the doyen of Nazi hunters, had stated publicly that he personally believed that Müller had escaped from Berlin and was still alive. As for the West Germans, they had put him back on their 'wanted' list ten years earlier and nominally he was still being sought by the Ludwigsburg office that dealt with such people. Yet in reality Müller was a dead issue. Was it because, thanks to the statements of Schellenberg*, Hoettl and Gehlen, the Western authorities believed that Müller had gone over to the Russians and there was no point in trying to find him in that sealed-off land?

According to Farago's account, Müller had adopted the identity of a young Gestapo man, Oskar Liedtke, 'tall, blond, blue-eyed, full of vim and patriotic', who had volunteered to go to the front to fight the Russians and had been killed in action in Russia in 1942. Müller, who was short, dark, brown-eyed, very careful with his energy and eighteen years older, had kept the dead man's papers. 'An idea flashed through his mind. Oskar was dead, but he could take on his identity. . . . The papers were appropriately retouched. . . . He took home the folder with the doctored documents and placed it in his private safe. He had it with him on 29 April 1945 when he was last seen alive, leaving the Führerbunker on his way back to his office on the Kurfürstenstrasse, where he now occupied Adolf Eichmann's supershelter.'

On 17 May, according to Farago, 'Müller left Berlin, going

---

* According to fellow Nazis, Schellenberg returned from one of his interrogations at Nuremberg to relate, 'I've really put one over them today (*dicke Birne aufgebunden*). I've told them [his US interrogators] that Müller went over to the Russians.'

west on the first leg of his escape'. He was dressed as an army private and accompanied by two companions, Heiden and Scholz. All he carried was a small suitcase 'packed with American dollar bills'.

Heiden, Farago relates, was arrested at a 'British checkpoint in Giessen'.* But after two weeks Müller and Scholz finally reached Munich, 'the first step on their original itinerary'. They stayed in Müller's old home town for three days. Apparently Müller didn't see his wife and children there, for as Frau Müller said afterwards, she had not seen her husband since December 1944, 'when he had me and the two children evacuated to Munich,' from their bombed house at Number 22 Corneliusstrasse 22, Berlin-Lankwitz.†

Three days later Müller and Scholz crossed into Austria near Mittenwald and headed for a safe house in the Fallmeyerstrasse in Innsbruck. Here a former employee of the Gestapo, Walter Brunner, was waiting for them. He was to be their guide till they reached Italy, where they would be taken over by an Italian waiting for them on the other side of the Brenner Pass at the 'Albergo Lupo' (the Wolf's Inn).

But the long journey through Austria, hopping from one remote village to the next along rough country tracks, proved too much for the escapee. 'By then the 45-year-old sedentary Müller, who walked with a limp and was suffering from fatigue, could take it no longer. The approach to the Brenner was too much for him and Müller had to return to Innsbruck.‡

In the end, after returning to Innsbruck for a rest, the unnamed organization taking care of the escapee handed him over to 'The Phantom of the Mountain' for assistance. He was Rudolf Blass, who had earned his nickname 'by being the ace among Austria's mountain guides'.

---

* There was no British checkpoint at Giessen, which was well within the US Zone of Occupation.
† Statement of Frau Müller to the German authorities in 1963. The house, a modest one, was still there when the author visited it in the late '80s.
‡ The 1940 picture of Müller and his mistress Anna in the Austrian mountains seems to contradict Farago's assertion that Müller wasn't up to tackling mountains. After all, as a Bavarian he had been brought up in a mountainous region.

A few months later (by September the snows would be falling heavily in the region, which wouldn't make Müller's ordeal any easier), according to Farago, Müller made it and 'reached Merano without a further hitch'.

'From there on, Müller travelled in style, no longer left to his own resources. . . . [He] was deposited at the Collegio Crotto on Piazzo Colonna, a seminary of Yugoslav priests who were adherents of Ante Pavelic, the deposed Nazi dictator of Croatia. After a few days at the Collegio, Father Mihailovic, superior of the seminary, took the former Gestapo chief to Grottaferrata to see the Titular Bishop of Aela, rector of the German Isituto Santa Maria dell' Anima, and one of the closest friends of Pope Pius II, whose Adjutant to the Throne he was. Contact was thus made with the Vatican rescue mission, which, in the person of Bishop Alois Hudal, assumed responsibility for Heinrich Müller's welfare from then on.'

Thus Farago involves the Vatican and indeed, indirectly, the whole of the Catholic Church in the rescue of Germany's second most wanted war criminal. Today it is clear that Pius XII, who was Papal Nuncio in Munich at the time that young Müller was beginning his police career, was more afraid of communism than he was of the new Nazi creed. It was said that, while he was in supposedly Catholic Munich, his pectoral cross was snatched from his breast by a 'Red' during the time of the Eisler revolution. It would only be natural, therefore, that he would order his subordinates to give aid and comfort to this important fugitive who had fought communism so long and so bravely, and, being a Bavarian, would be a good Catholic. Ironically enough, although Müller's wife and his parents were devout churchgoers, the Gestapo chief had made a formal application to leave the Catholic Church in the mid-thirties in order to further his career in a Party which eventually wanted to 'abolish' religion.*

Be that as it may, Müller was now, according to Farago, in the care of the most notorious of Croatia's fascist Catholic

---

* In Germany, then and now, one had to make a formal application to do this and thus avoid the *Kirchensteuer* (church tax) which is taken monthly from one's salary.

clergymen, whose activities in that country in the Second World War against the Greek Orthodox Serbs played a major role in influencing that later 'ethnic cleansing' of our own time.*

'By the time of Müller's visit in the summer of 1945,' Farago wrote, 'his mission had already handled hundreds of them [Nazi fugitives] who had made it to Rome. . . . [These Nazis], even Müller himself, had to be sheltered pending the completion of the arrangements for their departure. No questions were asked, no credentials had to be presented. Any name given was accepted. . . . This proved a complex and delicate task involving calculated risks. The Allied dragnet was out. Search parties of the security forces were combing Rome, picking up a fugitive Nazi here, a Fascist in hiding there, the Anglo-American teams working from lists of suspects with thousands of names on them.'

The 60-year-old 'Nazi Scarlet Pimpernel', as he was known in the Allied camp, finally obtained new false papers for Müller and his loyal companion, Scholz. According again to Farago, Müller became a Pole born in 1902 named Jan Belinski. Scholz was transformed into a Yugoslav named Dusko Stepanovic.

Living off the dollars that Müller had brought with him, they remained in Rome till they took the boat for South America in 1950. Was this long stay in Rome, exposed to the danger of being apprehended sooner or later by the pro-Allied Christian Democratic Italian Government, the reason for the cover story of the two graves in Berlin? Farago doesn't enlighten us. Instead he plunges on confidently with the rest of his story.

Ten years later Müller, now once again Oskar Liedtke, was working as an insurance salesman in Lima when he heard on 24 May 1960 that Eichmann had been kidnapped by *Mossad*. According to Farago, he took the news very seriously. He headed for the 'compound' belonging to his friend and fellow ex-Nazi Ferdinand Schwend, the only one in Peru who knew his real identity. The two were closeted together for hours. The result was that he returned to his Peruvian wife and sat

* Croatia was Germany's ally in the Second World War.

217

there, deep in thought, with his pistol on the table in front of him, as if he were considering suicide.

'The pistol was still there when his wife went looking for him in the morning and found the door to the den no longer locked. Müller was gone and so was "Oskar Liedtke" – for ever.'

The fugitive was driving at breakneck speed in his Volkswagen heading for the Bolivian border. Here, using a new passport in the name of 'Schreiker', given to him by Schwend, he crossed and disappeared for another twelve years when Schwend's compound was raided and a letter signed with the single letter 'H' and the postmark 'La Paz' was discovered. The pedantic Schwend had thoughtfully pencilled in on top of it 'Heinrich Müller' (or so Farago said), 'probably because he [Schwend] had so many aliases to remember that he wanted to be sure he had this one right.'

Müller was also listed in a little address book the raiders confiscated from Schwend's sister-in-law. 'There under "H Müller" was the notation "He now uses the name Herzog, lives near Cordoba in Argentina, managing a rabbit farm."'

As Farago concluded, without having produced a scrap of evidence for his account of Müller's career over the nearly two and a half decades since the latter had last been seen in Berlin, 'He is still there'.

Which is rather strange. For at that time he was resident in Albania, if he had not recently passed away after retiring from his command of that ultra-communist state's secret police.

For, according to half a dozen German journalists roused to action after the discovery in 1963 that the 'Müller grave' in the Berlin-Kreuzberg cemetery contained the bones of at least three different skeletons, none of them Müller's, the missing man had fled to a totally different refuge.

German author Peter Staehle had started the ball rolling in 1964. In that year he maintained in an article in the popular weekly *Der Stern* that Müller was to be found in the most backward state in Europe, Albania. According to Staehle, the Soviet authorities had indeed taken Müller from Berlin to Moscow. Here he had worked for the Soviets for ten years. In 1956, after a short time in Budapest, the KGB had sent him to

Tirana, the Albanian capital. Here, under the name of Abedin Bekir Nakoshire, he had formed and directed the local secret service's Western Intelligence section. Its efforts were mainly directed at Müller's old enemy, the British SIS, which was conducting an active campaign against the communists in that country, running in agents by sea and dropping them from the sky. (The British SIS officer who was in charge of this operation for a while was, incidentally, Kim Philby.)

Simon Wiesenthal, always a valuable source of information in such matters, readily agreed that Müller was definitely alive. He told the German *Frankfurter Rundschau* that he felt Müller would have gone east to the Russians, though he doubted somewhat that he was currently in Albania. Wiesenthal obviously thought that Albania was too much of a backwater for a man of Müller's talents.

Three years later, however, the Albanian connection was in the news once again. The West German *Neue Ruhr Zeitung* published the startling news that year that he was now living as a pensioner in Tirana. There he had taken up residence to enjoy a well-earned old age in the Villa Gorrice, which apparently belonged to the director of the local university library.

According to the West German newspaper, it had received its scoop from a German living in Italy, Helmut Lill. Back in 1949 he had been paid 400,000 Lire to smuggle Müller from Italy to Albania, which, since the Italian Army had occupied that country in 1940, had had fluctuating connections with the Italians, especially smugglers. According to Lill, Müller had then assumed the false name of Jergj Kovec. But who had paid Lill for his services the newspaper was unable to find out; it could have been Neo-Nazis or Moscow. It was a question that was never satisfactorily answered.

All the same, these wild stories about the fate of Müller did take a more serious and interesting turn in that year. For in November of 1967, when Helmut Lill sold his tale to the *Neue Ruhr Zeitung*, a robbery took place in Munich which seemed to indicate that one feared organization was taking an interest in the whereabouts of the missing Nazi for the first time.

THE MÜLLER FILE
FIVE

There is no denying that Munich has charm. Most German cities are clean, clinical – and ugly. The tower blocks, or 'dwelling silos' (*Wohnsilos*), as the Germans call them, might have colourful flower-boxes on their spotless balconies, but they are still highrise brick boxes. Munich is different. Here there are pretty central markets, parks and cafes where handsome, well-dressed young people seem to have all the time in the world to chat, make eyes and drink that excellent *Löwenbrau* beer.

For the inhabitants of the 'Free State of Bavaria' want their fellow Germans and the rest of the world to know that they are different from the rest of Germany. They have their own life style. They are not as *'Bierernst'* (as serious as beer) as the rest of their countrymen. After all, it was those 'damned sow-Prussians' who started Germany's wars of the last century. Up there in Berlin, that's where the trouble has always come from, not here in Munich.

But the Bavarian alibi does not really wash, as far as the Second World War is concerned. For it was in Munich that Hitler learned his anti-semitism in the immediate post-First World War years. Munich saw the foundation of Drexler's German Workers' Party which, as Hitler often lied, he turned into the Nazi Party 'with only seven men'. In those years Munich became the home of all the key figures – Goering, Himmler, Hess, Heydrich – who were to run the National Socialist Workers' Party which took over Germany

223

and led that country into the Second World War in 1939.

But a year earlier, in 1938, Munich had been the site of the meeting between 'Herr Hitler', as British Premier Neville Chamberlain always called the Führer, himself and the French prime minister Daladier. Thanks to Chamberlain and his 'peace in our time', Munich will always be synonymous with betrayal. Perhaps it was, therefore, right and proper that Munich became the place where the only serious attempt was ever made to really find out what happened to its infamous son Müller.

On the night of 3 November 1967 two men broke into the home of Frau Sophie Müller at Number Four Manzinger Weg in the suburb of Munich-Pasing. As it was later reported in that excellent Munich paper *die Süddeutsche Zeitung*, both the burglars, if that was what they really were, were equipped with radios and flash cameras: unusual equipment for two men intent on robbing an unpretentious house.

That night Frau Müller, still officially married to Heinrich, though now regarded as a widow, was in hospital. She was 67 years old, had a hard life behind her, especially after the war when she had to struggle as the wife of a major war criminal, with two children to feed, and was beginning to feel her years. But the robbers hadn't reckoned with the curiosity of the typical German suburban housewife. They were spotted. The neighbours called the police and before the two men could escape the Bavarian police had sprung out of their green-and-white BMWs.

The men were obviously foreigners, but that was nothing new. All German cities at that time were full of 'guest workers' (*Gastarbeiter*) who spoke shaky German. But these two didn't work in Germany. Their employers were Israelis. For one of the arrested men was very careless. The police searching him found a wage strip in a language they couldn't identify at once. In fact, it was in Hebrew and, as the Munich *Abendzeitung* put it discreetly, indicated that two foreigners were working for 'a secret organization . . . located in Israel'. In other words, the two men, Baruch Shur, aged 39, from Tel Aviv, and Daniel Gordon, aged 38, from Haifa, were employees of the *Mossad*!

The Munich District Attorney's office ordered the men to be held without bail while the investigation continued into this strange event. Naturally there were many other Israelis in West Germany. Indeed in the '60s and '70s that country, surprisingly enough, became a modest Mecca for Jews, many of whom were engaged in show business and the new night clubs which were beginning to spring up everywhere. Among them, as was to be expected, there were a few crooks, but rarely common-or-garden housebreakers. Even rarer were the latter employed by the *Mossad*.

Now the Israelis' diplomatic representation in Bonn stepped in and hired crack lawyer Rolf Bossi to defend the two accused. A new dimension was added to the whole strange business when it was discovered during the preparations for the trial that both the Israelis were officials of their state. In other words, the two were *Mossad* agents, who had broken into the Frau Müller house, armed with highly unusual tools for burglars – cameras and radios.*

It was clear that this had been a carefully planned operation, involving more than the two arrested men. Somewhere there had been a get-away car involved too, but perhaps the well-known wail of the 'Martin's horn', the German police siren, had sent the other agents scurrying for cover.

Bossi had two tasks: one, to get the two agents off; two, to ensure that the Israeli government was not involved. That government had been criticized enough for having kidnapped Eichmann seven years before and there had been several ugly incidents of a diplomatic nature. The Israelis could not risk another run-in with the Bonn Government, which had done so much to pay for the establishment of the Jewish state in the early '50s. As cynical German politicians in Bonn were wont to quip, 'One day the Jews will put up a statue of Adolf in Jerusalem's main square'.

Bossi, for the defence, took the approach of disassociating the would-be robbers from the Israeli Government. The two men had acted without orders and independently of *Mossad*.

---

* The latter indicated that they had not been alone before they had been arrested; they had been in radio contact with other agents.

They had been motivated by 'emotional reasons'. In some way or other, Bossi never made it quite clear, they wanted to wreak a kind of revenge on the missing Müller.

When Simon Wiesenthal was called on to comment, as he usually was in such matters, he told the Munich *Abendzeitung*, 'They really got themselves in a pickle', meaning the two agents. Then he changed the subject and, as the paper put it, 'gave the authorities a tip . . . which is being followed up by the authorities at Ludwigsburg'. As Wiesenthal saw it, Müller had managed to get away from Berlin in '45. Further, he knew that Müller was in Egypt, then Israel's main enemy, and that he had 'a contact person' in Munich. As the paper concluded, that 'contact person' with Müller was the reason for the break-in attempt.

It was a defence that the two *Mossad* agents used too. They had acted off their own bat – '*aus emotionellen Motiven*' – and not their bosses. It was then that Israel's General Consulate in Bad Godesberg stated it was prepared to put up a bond of DM 15,000 for the two agents.

But the bond didn't suffice. The Germans were beginning to get tough with Israel. A spokesman for the Bavarian Ministry of Justice told the Swiss paper *Die Neue Züriche Zeitung* that the incident was causing 'diplomatic difficulties' between the Federal Republic and Israel. The Ministry was about to issue a new warrant against Shur and Gordon, not only for attempted burglary but also for conspiracy and abuse of the *Ausländergesetz* (Foreigners' Law). The *Abendzeitung* joined in. Its editor sharply criticized the two Israeli agents for infringing the Federal Republic's sovereignty. The right-wing Neo-Nazi *Deutsche Nationale Zeitung* said that the case reminded it of the 'Eichmann Kidnapping'. The Bavarians were showing themselves in their true colours; they weren't so laid back as they seemed to be.

The case began to escalate. The German government started to worry. They had to think of Germany's flourishing export trade, especially with the USA. One of the agents being interrogated then let slip that they hadn't after all tried to break into Frau Müller's house under their own steam. It appeared they had been 'under orders'. The information was leaked. Now the German government decided it was time to bring an end to the whole unfortunate business. Dr Spietzer, Berlin's first district attorney, interrogated the two *Mossad* agents and afterwards stated they had been justified, to a certain extent, in their illegal actions. It was time for Spietzer, as representative of Berlin, to co-operate more closely with the Israeli authorities.

Three weeks after that interrogation, obviously instigated by an embarrassed Bonn government, Shur and Gordon were sentenced to three months' imprisonment. They were taken to Roehm's old prison in Munich-Stadelheim to serve their sentence. But they didn't stay behind bars long. Shortly thereafter they were quietly deported and no more was heard of the matter. A decade later Frau Müller was dead, taking whatever secrets she might have possessed about her husband with her to the grave.

Thereafter, it seems that no serious search was ever made for the missing head of the Gestapo. 'The Man Without Shadows' had vanished for good.*

* In theory Müller is still on the German wanted list as a war criminal. If he is still alive, he is now a hundred years old.

FINALE

'Those who were caught by the great illusion of our time, and have lived through its intellectual and moral debauch, either give themselves up to a new addiction of the opposite type or are condemned to pay with a lifelong hangover.'

Arthur Koestler: *The God That Failed.*

In 1918 Vice-Sergeant Heinrich Müller of the Imperial Army's *Flieger-Abteilung 287* took off in his rickety old wire-and-canvas bomber from one of the German Air Force's fields in French Lorraine. German troops were still advancing in their last decisive offensive westwards, tackling first the British Fifth Army and then the French. Back in Spa, General-Quartermaster Ludendorff, who had planned this do-or-die attack on the Allies, knew his armies had little time left. If they didn't crush the Anglo-French resistance and reach the Channel soon, the new US Army would take up the challenge and that would be it. America had hundreds of thousands of fresh, keen young men, unaffected by war-weariness like the European armies who had been fighting for four long years. As the Germans said, it was *'Marsch oder krepieren'* (March or croak).

That late spring the 18-year-old Bavarian pilot from Munich might have felt the same sense of urgency. For on this May day Heinrich Müller was going to undergo his only few hours of danger. Alone and without escort, he was setting off in his unwieldy bomber to carry out a solo mission. It was of the kind that the Germans knew as a *'Himmelfahrtskommando'* (an Ascension Day operation) i.e. a one-way mission. For the 18-year-old behind the wooden steering wheel was going to bomb Paris. In the whole forty-five accountable years of his life until May 1945 this was the only time that the future head of the Gestapo was to play the role of a man of action.

231

The details of his solo attack on the French capital, braving the rings of anti-aircraft guns which, even in those days, defended Paris, are obscure, but it is clear from the official Imperial reaction to the youngster's bravery that he carried out his self-imposed mission well. He was immediately awarded a decoration that was rarely given to non-commissioned officers for outstanding courage, the Iron Cross, First Class.* That was followed by the Bavarian 'Military Service Cross with Crown and Swords', plus another Iron Cross and a couple of other Royal Bavarian decorations. In due course, Müller would return home to marry Sofie Dischner, the girl he had met in Munich the year before.

The award of the Iron Cross marked the end of Müller's career as a man of action. From now on he would be tied to a desk. He'd become the classic civil servant, whose active role was limited to signing orders carried out by those in the field. He'd turn out to become what post-war generations of Germans would call *die Schreibtischtäter* (the writing-desk killers): those who absolved themselves from the crimes carried out on their orders by other men.

Müller would be far removed from the dirt, the blood and the sheer horror of the ghettos, the concentration camps and the Russian PoW cages. For the rest of his police career he would work behind his big desk in Berlin, signing and shuffling papers eleven or twelve hours a day, six days a week. Officially his pen would be tipped in orange ink†, but really it was dipped in blood!

But at night he would return home to a comfy, warm bed, with, if he was lucky, a plump female companion or his wife to cuddle, if he chose, and forget the problems of his working day. For him and his like there would be no violent action.

Now, however, on this day of defeat, 2 May 1945, with the Führer dead and the whole established order which had

---

* For instance, the sergeant who first entered and eventually captured Fort Douaumont in Verdun received the same award for his outstanding bravery in taking such an important objective.

† In the Gestapo hierarchy pecking-order, each of the top officials had a different coloured ink for signing orders. Müller's was orange.

cushioned him from the harsh realities of total war destroyed, he realized that a phase in his life had come to an end. After a quarter of a century of sedentary life, first in Munich and then in Berlin, he was faced with an overwhelming decision. As he hid there among the smoking ruins of the conquered capital, he had to commit himself either to violent action, if he wished to survive, or to die.

When he had last seen his mistress Anna in the ruins of his bombed house in the Corneliusstrasse in Berlin-Lankwitz, they had burned certain private papers, which Anna had taken as a sign that her lover was about to disappear. But Heinrich had told her that was not to be the case. He said, in her words, 'In view of the catastrophic situation that he couldn't and wouldn't go on. . . . The better men had won.'

That had roused her disbelief and she retorted, 'You can't mean that the Russians are better than us!'

According to his mistress, who was eighteen years younger than he, Müller had nodded and said, 'Yes, they are.' He then had added that he had just come from a last conference at that infamous house on the Wannsee where the Final Solution had been decided upon. Somehow she had felt that there the *final decisions* had been made too, about Müller and the rest of the Gestapo and SD chiefs. She had been depressed by her lover's fatalistic mood and, according to her own words, she 'had gone down' on her knees and 'begged him to make a run for it'. But she felt that they had had no effect and that her lover was resigned to his fate.

But was he still, on this May day two weeks later?

It is clear that Müller had definitely made preparations for an escape from Berlin in an emergency previous to this time. He had had false papers prepared, though whether they were the ones that Farago has mentioned, issued in the name of his dead assistant, Oskar Liedtke, is doubtful. We know, too, that Müller and other Gestapo chiefs had prepared a provisional new *Gestapo HQ Süd* in the Bavaria town of Hof.

Here in the village of Koeditz outside Hof, at the Villa Hobuehl, *SS Obersturmführer* Duchstein had taken charge of a special headquarters, code-named 'Badger' (*Dachs*), where in due course 'two large suitcases' labelled 'SS Gruppenführer Müller' had arrived. There, shortly before his meeting with his mistress, he had called briefly after inspecting the main Gestapo HQ at Hof.*

So it seems that Müller might have been preparing his flight to the village of Koeditz at the same time as he was investigating the 'leak' in the Bunker. We know that at times he still seemed to be thinking positively on that day when he met his mistress, and she pleaded with him not to lose heart. For on the same day another of Müller's adjutants, Schuhmacher, was urged by his boss to ensure that the other group of the Gestapo, which intended to set up in the north in the region of the 'Doenitz Enclave' (*Gestapo-Nord*), 'got cracking and into the trucks'. As the latter recorded after the war, 'I met Müller for the last time near his private dwelling at Berlin-Lankwitz outside the railway station there. After telling me to hurry up the people heading north, he said he was staying behind. He had been ordered by the Führer to remain in Berlin.'

This is doubtful. The Führer had other things on his mind than Gestapo Müller. Still it and other discussions he held at that time indicate that he was still capable of making logical and purposeful decisions. Had his attitude totally changed since the last half of April? Naturally he had seen and experienced some terrible things in the intervening period. He had executed Hitler's brother-in-law Fegelein on the former's orders. He had been in the area when the Führer had killed his new wife and then had committed suicide. He had seen the top people of the Reich fall apart in the Bunker. Now, on 2 May, he was experiencing the end of resistance in Central Berlin.

The Russians had won. Those of the *Prominenz* who could had fled. Those who were left in the Bunker and its immediate

---

* The place was later captured by French troops, who looted it and took Müller's suitcases with them. What treasure trove they might have contained! Today some of their contents may well be up for sale in some dusty North African *souk*, for the 'liberators' of Hof were mainly colonial soldiers from France's then North African colonies.

surrounding area were the dead, the drunk and the defeatists. Could Müller be classified as one the latter?

We have already examined the various escape routes open to him. We know, too, that two graves did not contain his remains, as was said at the time. We have eye-witness statements on his whereabouts till about the late afternoon of that 2 May, ie in the general area of the Bunker. So what could have happened between his last sighting and his 'supposed' burial in the graves, which, as we have seen, is not correct?

For three months, from May till August 1945, there is no mention in the official records kept at the time – and we must remember that Germany was in a state of chaos that summer and, as far as Berlin was concerned, the Russians ruled the roost. They could censor, alter or fake 'official' records in any way they wished.

In August, however, the authorities dispatched a group of former German PoWs to clear away the dead, mostly buried by now in makeshift graves, in the former government quarter. They didn't want decaying bodies spreading epidemics. One of these PoWs, a former medical orderly like many of his comrades, came across a corpse in a general's uniform. It was buried in a single grave in the grounds of Goering's Air Force Ministry.* In the pocket, the PoW, whose name was Walter Lueders, was found an identity card in the name of Heinrich Müller. Thereupon the corpse was dispatched for burial at the cemetery in the *Grosse Hamburger Strasse*, as we already know. From the old Jewish cemetery, 'Müller's' body was exhumed and transferred on 15 September 1945 to its final resting place. However, it was not officially identified as Müller's body by retired Detective Inspector Fritz Leopold till three months later on 15 December 1945. Thereupon an identification marker, made of metal, was placed on the grave until it was finally replaced by the marble stone, presumably paid for and tended by Anna, the dead man's mistress.

So one minor mystery is now cleared up. It was not old

* The Air Ministry is still in use, now by a ministry of the German government recently moved from Bonn to Berlin.

comrades or Neo-Nazis who looked after 'Müller's' grave until it was finally opened up nearly twenty years later to reveal that it didn't contain the bones of the long-supposed dead Gestapo boss but the remains of at least three other skeletons.

However, we still have that six-month period between May and December 1945 when Müller was not accounted for and the rumours about his survival and subsequent flight started. When Heinz Pannwitz, who had run the Gestapo's 'radio game' with Moscow from Paris till 1944, was questioned by his KGB interrogators after the war, the subject turned to Müller. In that year, 1947, Pannwitz was told by the Russian secret servicemen that Müller's corpse had been found in the summer of 1945 in Berlin. They had discovered the dead men in the tunnel at the capital's underground station of Kaiserhof.

According to Pannwitz the Russians said that Müller had committed suicide. Their agents had taken his official documents, identification papers etc. These, Pannwitz maintained after his release from Soviet captivity in 1955, he had seen. They also included Müller's photos, and it was for this reason that the identification documents sent to Frau Müller in Munich in December/January 1945–1946 were minus their photographs.

Be that as it may, Pannwitz states that the Russians knew Müller was dead and had not gone over to them, as so many of his enemies maintained after the war. This was supported by Müller's friends, such as his old colleague from Bavarian Police/Gestapo days, *Kommissar* Huber, and naturally his mistress, Anna. They didn't want to believe that after fighting the communists for so long he had finally gone over to them. What value could they then place on all those years when he had been their scourge? Had he been a traitor and hypocrite all along?

It is obvious that Pannwitz's story had holes in it. Besides, as a penniless ex-Nazi former prisoner of the Russians, he might have made the whole thing up to earn money from newspapers always eager to publish sensations. All the same, even if we assume that Müller *did* die in that underground tunnel at Kaiserhof and one of the Germans involved in

236

clearing up had handed over the dead man's papers to the Russians, what became of the body?

As we know, his official grave does not contain his remains. What about the original one in which Walter Lueders maintained he buried the body of an SS *Gruppenführer* with the ID of Heinrich Müller, found in the grounds of Goering's Air Ministry (not the underground tunnel, as Pannwitz's story had it)? Nearly twenty years later, when interrogated by Berlin's police, he still stuck to that original story. But there was a catch. By 1963 Lueders couldn't remember *exactly* where the spot was in which he had found the body, nor where *exactly* it had been interred in the Old Jewish Cemetery.

In September 1973, at the same time that a spokesman for Paramount in Hollywood announced that his studios had bought the rights to Ladislas Farago's book, in which he described how he personally had met *Reichsleiter* Bormann in the jungles of Paraguay the year before, Dr Richter of the West German judicial system released the following statement to the media:

'The burial of the skeleton of *Reichsleiter* Bormann, found on 7/8 December in Berlin(West) on the terrain of the Ulap site in the Invalidenstrasse, is authorized. Cremation is not to be allowed.'*

After nearly twenty years, Bormann had been found at last. 'But where had the body been all that time? In the same place in the *Invalidenstrasse*, where ex-German Post Office worker, one Albert Krumnow, had always maintained he had buried it on 2 May 1945. All the time the skeleton had been lying there with that of Dr Stumpfegger, a mere ten metres from where Krumnow had been sure he'd buried them so long before and never been believed.

Could something similar have happened to the remains of

* So that, in case of doubt, the skeleton could always be dug up again. Later, when it appeared that the site might become a place of pilgrimage for Neo-Nazis as Hess's grave has become, it was said that the remains were cremated after all and the ash dropped into the North Sea from a plane.

Müller? After all they were transferred and only certified as those of the missing man three months later, when they must have been decomposed, especially since they had not been buried in a proper coffin in the summer of 1945. Did retired Detective Inspector Leopold take a quick look and hastily identify Müller on the basis of the documents forwarded with the remains? Perhaps he didn't even look at them – a collection of human bits and pieces which turned out to be the remains of three separate and never identified soldiers, all much younger than Müller, aged 45 in 1945.

Had, in other words, the long dead Walter Lueders been right after all? As he testified in 1963: 'I saw his pass [*Ausweis*] with my own eyes and I remember that this pass was made out in the name of Heinrich Müller'. Is it a fact that the skeleton of Heinrich Müller still remains in roughly the same area where Lueders swore he buried him over a half a century ago?

It would be a supreme irony of the history of our time that the remains of Heinrich Müller, the co-author of the Final Solution, the scourge of the Jews, lies buried in what was once Berlin's Old Jewish Cemetery.

APPENDIX

The Last of Gestapo Müller . . . Or?

Zentrale Stelle
der Landesjustizverwaltungen

- 110 AR 346/2000 -

Bei Antwortschreiben Aktenzeichen angeben!

Zentrale Stelle   Postfach 11 44   71611 Ludwigsburg

71638 Ludwigsburg, den **31. 01. 2000**
Schorndorfer Straße 58
Fernsprechanschluß:
Ludwigsburg Nr. (0 71 41) 18-9
bei Durchwahl 18 App. **6215**

Telefax:
(0 71 41) 18 62 17

MÜLLER soll lt. Sterbeurkunde des Standesamtes Berlin-Mitte
- 11706/45 - verstorben sein. Eine andere Version (siehe hier
110 AR 1619/97) besagt: "Müller soll in den letzten Kriegs-
tagen in Berlin nicht ums Leben gekommen, sondern in die
Schweiz entkommen sein. Dort soll er zunächst untergetaucht
sein, bis ihn der amerikanische Geheimdienst ausfindig gemacht
hat. Er sei in die USA gebracht worden, habe die amerikanische
Staatsbürgerschaft und einen neuen Namen bekommen und in einer
speziellen antikommunistischen Aufklärungsgruppe d. CIA, die
unmittelbar vom Weissen Haus aus gesteuert worden sein soll,
gearbeitet (in den Jahren 1948 - 1951). Dann soll er im Range
eines Armeegenerals in Pension gegangen sein, geheiratet und
noch zwei Kinder bekommen haben und im Jahre 1973 unbehelligt
von weiteren Nachforschungen in den USA verstorben sein.

Letzte Klarheit wird wohl kaum zu erlangen sein.

Mit freundlichen Grüßen

239

Translation

Another version states that Müller didn't die in Berlin in the last days of the war. Instead he fled to Switzerland. Here he went 'underground' until he was discovered by the US Secret Service. He was taken to the States, given US citizenship and a new name. Here he specialized in anti-communism, under the auspices of the CIA. This group was directly controlled by the White House (1948–1951). Thereafter he was pensioned off with the rank of general. He married again and fathered two children, dying in 1973, unbothered by any further investigations.

With friendly greetings . . .'

Communication to the author from the Central Office of State Justice, Ludwigsburg, Bavaria. 31.1.2000. This office had dealt with the investigation of the fate of the missing Nazi war criminals since the foundation of the German Federal Republic in 1949.

INDEX

241